ALL FOR THE BEST

ALL FOR THE BEST
Testimonies of Christian growth

compiled by Stewart Dinnen

WEC PUBLICATIONS, Gerrards Cross

First published 1988.

British Library Cataloguing in Publication Data
All for the best : testimonies of Christian growth.
1. Experience (Religion)
I. Dinnen, Stewart
248.2   BR110

ISBN 0-900828-46-3

WEC PUBLICATIONS,
Bulstrode, Oxford Road,
Gerrards Cross, Bucks, SL9 8SZ

Unless otherwise stated Scripture quotations in this publi-cation are from The Holy Bible, New International Version, Copyright © 1973, 1978, International Bible Society.

Cover design by John Tromans

PRINTED OFFSET LITHO IN GREAT BRITAIN
BY WEC PRESS, GERRARDS CROSS, BUCKS.

Contents

Contents

INTRODUCTION

Stuck? Want to be moving and maturing? Or perhaps you *are* moving and it's so exciting you want to move *faster*!

If you are saying "Yes" to any part of that first paragraph this book could well meet your need.

It contains a number of accounts of how people have advanced in their walk with God — their fears, their fumblings, and their movement towards vital faith.

They are rewarding stories because they are honest, down-to-earth testimonies about things that are usually left up in the air. You'll be able to 'get a handle' on the particular aspect of truth illustrated.

Each chapter contains vital spiritual principles. Some are highlighted for you before you move on to a new chapter, so don't rush through. Let the Spirit of truth take the principles and apply them directly and deeply to your own life.

You never grow simply by *knowing*. You grow when you take what you have learned and *apply* it with the will. In algebraic terms:

K (knowledge) $+$ **A** (application) $=$ **G** (growth)

The mind and the will have to be in action together, and when that happens you have the experience of being liberated by truth. Try it!

Stewart Dinnen
Gerrards Cross
January 1987

SECTION 1

THE END OF ME —

GOD TAKES OVER

1

MY DESERT — AND HIS OASIS

'Martje van de Berg'
(Proper names have been altered
in the interests of security.)

Destination Desert

Fierce-looking tribesmen watched us as we landed in 'Khamzan' on a clear summer day in 1972. Stray dogs kept a safe distance. Birds of prey soared high above a dusty plain which ended in rugged mountains.

I felt as if I were entering a different world. Only the white baby coat of our one-year-old son reminded me vaguely of the clean and orderly world we had left behind. But even that memory was fleeting; the dirty airport floors had long lost their original whiteness.

We had entered a different world indeed! This was a world ruled by strong family bonds, tribal allegiances and blood feuds; a world where honour and bravery are considered higher virtues than truth, love and compassion.

We had come to set up and run a small hospital in an area devoid of any medical care. With our arrival a long-fostered dream had become true.

It wasn't long before that dream seemed completely shattered. I am embarrassed to have to admit that our problems in the first couple of years were more related to learning to work together as a mission team, than to living in a strange culture.

Our leaders were a couple with experience in the Muslim world. They were naturally anxious to see the project succeed in conservative and potentially hostile surroundings, so they left us little room to fool around. The other six of us were all new recruits, somewhat immature, critical in outlook, and rather unbroken, I'm afraid. Different cultural backgrounds, strong views, cramped living conditions and few social outlets created an ideal climate for clashes. Soon my husband and I felt ill at ease and not accepted. The fact that I was pregnant again and not feeling well increased my inability to cope. We thought back on God's guidance in our lives. Had we somehow misunderstood His direction?

Happier days in Holland

I had been a happy and secure child who loved the Lord and wanted to serve Him. As a teenager I had joined a Bible club, which provided me with a circle of Christian friends. Not only did we hike, swim, and play football on the beach, we also met every Saturday evening for Bible study, and on Sunday morning early for a prayer meeting. Deep and lasting friendships were made while we searched together to discover how we could serve the Lord.

At the age of seventeen I participated in a summer campaign organised by Operation Mobilisation. It was a revolutionary experience. A lot of my theoretical Christian knowledge became practical. It was also in OM that I was confronted with the challenge of Islam. I was sure that I was to be a missionary, and most likely among Muslims.

In my final year of grammar school I sought further direction. I had an aptitude for mathematics and science, and was interested in studying medicine, but the length of the study discouraged me somewhat. When I consulted various people I got conflicting advice. One morning I read James 1:5: "If any of you lacks wisdom, he should ask God who gives generously to all ..." I took this promise, and in the wisdom I believed I had received, I decided to become a doctor, enrolling in the rather leftist University of Amsterdam.

Later I met Hans, a medical student two years my senior, who shared the same desire to serve God in the Muslim world. Even before graduation we started looking for job opportunities abroad. We approached several mission boards related to our church but found out that they had no work in the part of the world in which we were interested. In 1970 we attended a mission conference put on by various faith missions. Here the challenge of Khamzan was presented — an open door for medical professionals in a strongly Islamic country. We both knew that this was God's call to us, and this assurance grew as time went by.

Our steps were directed towards WEC International, one of the societies considering entrance into Khamzan. During the Candidate Course we became acquainted with the mission's working principles and we came to love and appreciate the praying and supportive fellowship within the WEC Family.

Seeing it through

So, we really had no reason to doubt God's clear guidance, and by God's grace we did not quit. Our home background of strong dykes, adverse winds and Calvinism helped us to stick it out!

A holiday away from the place of tension greatly helped us to see things in proper perspective. Many issues were not that important after all! I also came to see myself in a new and not too flattering light. I discovered that I was oversensitive and critical, and that the 'beam' of criticism in my own eye considerably distorted my view, both of fellow workers and of the situation.

One of WEC's international leaders came out to counsel our team, and gradually things began to work out. We learned to relate to and appreciate one another. Mutual trust was built, and fellowship restored.

After these initial problems we settled in quite well. The fierce tribespeople turned out to be warm and loyal friends, once we got to know them. As the men began to trust us, they started to bring their wives to the clinic. If a Khamzani woman fails to produce living children, her husband may divorce her, or at least take a second wife. How gratifying to help a woman have her first living baby after eight pregnancies!

We became accustomed to the fact that Khamzanis don't like to leave a patient alone in hospital. Often several relatives or friends stay with him, cooking his favourite food in the corridor and sometimes even sharing the bed with him! If the patient is a victim of blood revenge, as many as twenty or thirty armed men from his village or tribe keep watch around the hospital, turning it into a kind of fortress. Once the patient is discharged, we often get an invitation for a meal in his home. Nothing can be compared with the famous Khamzani hospitality! These visits give us opportunities to build friendships and share the gospel.

In the early days of the medical work we had to tackle anything, often with limited resources. As time went by and our facilities improved, we were able to help the patients more effectively. Life was full of challenge, and although we did not work for men's appreciation, we received plenty of it.

My personal desert

In 1977 our third child was born after a troublesome pregnancy. Little Annette was only four pounds, but right from birth she was a fighter. She made it all right! She has a great sense of humour and infectious laughter.

But by now we had become field leaders. Hans was the only full-time doctor, being on duty day and night, seven days a week. The work kept multiplying and gradually exhaustion crept in. He continued to do all he had to do but, when he finally got home at night, he had little or no energy left to contribute anything to our family life. Our different personalities started to play up. Hans is a reserved type of person, and when he gets tired he withdraws within himself and becomes very quiet. To me verbal expression is almost as much a necessity of life as breathing! I started to feel emotionally neglected. I guess I was. We tried to talk things out. We prayed about it. We started to quarrel about it! These quarrels would often leave me crying. The more I pressed Hans, the more he withdrew.

I went over the happy memories of our first love, as one looks at pictures from times long past, or places far removed. We had met during one of the summer campaigns with Operation Mobilisation. I felt much attracted to Hans' quiet reserve. He seemed so strong and controlled, compared to my outgoing and rather impulsive nature. On one of the last days of that summer we went for a walk in the woods. Hans confided that he knew a great many girls (probably a bit of an overstatement, but who cares), but that he had never experienced what he felt for me. He was quite sure that the Lord wanted us to continue our lives together. I had been often 'in love' since I was fourteen and needed time to sort out my feelings. Soon I was as sure as he was, and our relationship proved durable. Halfway through my study we got married. Happy and busy years followed as Hans graduated and worked as a resident in a hospital to get more experience in the fields of internal medicine, surgery and obstetrics. When I graduated in 1971, we were the proud parents of a beautiful baby.

Together we had made our mud house in Khamzan into a home. Hans had taken some share in the care of the children to enable me to be involved in the medical work as well. We had sweated together over our first emergencies as Hans operated and I gave the anaesthetic. We had been companions in joy and laughter, in disappointment, hurt and sickness. Now our common adventure seemed to have turned against us.

A new perspective

In this dark episode God met me, not by changing the circumstances, but by changing my perspective. He showed me that I had placed myself in the centre of my thinking; *I* was neglected, *my* emotional needs were not met. But He did not ask me to put Hans in the centre either! That place had to be given back to Him. My prayer changed from, "Lord, let Hans be more communicative and meet my emotional needs," to, "Make Hans and me people who please You."

I discovered that the romantic expectation I entertained, that my husband could meet all my emotional needs, was somewhat unrealistic. God provided other means to meet my needs, such as rewarding friendships with lady colleagues. And as I relaxed, our relationship improved, and new affection sprang up. In 1980 we had our first long furlough, which gave us the much needed time to rest and unwind.

Five more years have passed.

We have a number of fine and dedicated fellow-workers, including two doctors. Our two older children attend an international high school in the capital and live away from home most of the year. We've gone deeper into the culture and language and have developed warm friendships with Khamzani people. There are regular opportunities to share the good news and hand out scriptures.

But there are still some battles to be fought. With growing opportunities there is also growing opposition to our presence. Time and again false accusations are brought against us. The threat of expulsion is always lurking around the corner.

For a couple of years the medical work has been completely under Khamzani administration and we have to depend on the often deficient supplies of the Ministry of Health. Some of our professional (non-Christian) colleagues ask for large amounts of money for their rather poor services. How easy to get a negative or complaining attitude in such circumstances! The apostle James tells us to consider it pure joy, whenever we face trials of many kinds, because we know that the testing of our faith develops perseverance. Perseverance must finish its work, so that we may be mature and complete, not lacking anything. What a challenge!

So we continue to be learners in this adventure, trusting God for the ultimate outcome.

Points to Ponder:
1. Who or what is at the centre of your world?
2. Are circumstances getting on top of you? What *practical* steps can you take to relieve the situation?

Relevant scriptures:
1. Psalm 34:1-8, Romans 11:36.
2. Psalm 42:5-6, Mark 6:30-32, 2 Corinthians 2:12-14.

2

MY SUCCESS – OR HIS SUFFICIENCY?

Keith Bergmeier

Overcoming

"Excuse me, Dona Mercedes, but this girl has done her essay in English!" After arriving in Spain before the summer holidays we had enrolled our two girls, Victoria and Heidi (then eight and five), in local Spanish state schools. During the holidays they had mixed with their friends in the street and had learned to communicate in Spanish fairly well.

Now it was September and the first day of school in a new country. The first assignment was for all the children to write an account of what they had done during the holidays. Victoria had never written in Spanish before so, doing the only thing possible, wrote in English. The principal had forgotten to inform the teacher that she would have a 'foreigner' in her class. So, when Dona Mercedes was informed of the anomaly, she threw her hands in the air and went into a panic. Some harsh words were thrown in Victoria's direction, with the result that she arrived home in tears.

It is hard to describe how we felt for our daughter at that time. We were the ones who had left New Zealand to come and do God's will, but now it seemed that our little girl was suffering for it! The doubts began to set in. Had we done the right thing sending her to a Spanish school? How could we send her back to face the same thing tomorrow?

All those 'helpful' comments from well-meaning friends at home began to ring in our ears. "I think it's cruel to take children to a foreign country." "Don't you realise that they will be away from their grandparents?" "It will be difficult for them to study in Spanish schools." And, of course, there had always been our own natural fears as well.

We had some earnest prayer, and both dad and mum accompanied Victoria to school the next day. Dona Mercedes seemed somewhat repentant as we talked about the situation and asked if there was anything that we could do to help. She put her arm around Victoria and, speaking more like a regimented German than a typical Spaniard, said, "Victoria *will* be my special friend. I *will* teach her Spanish and she *will* write perfectly in one month."

In six weeks Victoria did all her exams in Spanish and was among the top in the class! Dona Mercedes taught her for three years and became a very special friend. We could not have wanted for a better teacher.

As we follow God's leading He shows us that we need to listen only to Him, and not to the doubts and fears which come, directly or indirectly, from the enemy.

But let me go back and tell you how we came to be missionaries in Spain.

Growing

Born in Melbourne, Australia, I spent most of my youth in Northern Victoria where my parents were dairy farmers. I was raised as a Presbyterian and, along with the rest of my family, made my first response to the gospel in 1962, during an evangelistic crusade organised by the local churches in my home town.

Six months later, when I was fifteen, I left school and began taking evening classes in accounting, while working as a clerk during the day. In 1969 I completed my studies and in early 1970 travelled to New Zealand where I met Fay, who was to become my wife a year later. By this time worldly ambition and liberal teaching in the church had dimmed any spiritual experience that I had ever had.

Motivated by the birth of our first daughter, we began to attend a Presbyterian church and found people with a living faith that was so contagious that we soon caught it too. This resulted in a full surrender of my life to the Lord, and a search for His specific will in the service of His Kingdom.

In 1976 I resigned my management consulting job to respond to God's call and we went as a family to the WEC Missionary Training College in Tasmania. During our time of training God put before us the spiritual need of the Spanish people. In Spain we had our initial language study and cultural orientation in the Mediterranean city of Valencia, then stayed on to work there until the middle of 1984.

Adjusting

It was hot, so we stopped for an ice cream. We had been evangelising in the park for an hour or so, talking to ones and twos. This is a common activity in our church-planting programme in Madrid. We decided to relax and enjoy the fresh air.

As we were deciding whether to have orange or lemon, Fay noticed an elderly lady reading a black-covered book which was lying open on the counter of the little stall. "Are you studying something?" I asked. "No, I'm trying to learn how to pray," was the reply. (She was reading a Catholic prayer book.)

So began a long and spontaneous discussion. We discovered that this lady, who had suffered much hardship in her life, was sincerely seeking God. She was the proprietress of the ice cream stall, and when another worker, Liz, appeared on the scene to talk with her daughter (also selling ice cream) Rafaela poured out her heart to us. She was touched by the reality of a Christian testimony.

Three months later, Rafaela eagerly welcomed the women of our team into her house to study the Bible, pray, and listen to cassettes. A lovely friendship was formed.

So often in 'traditional' evangelism we hit our heads against brick walls, and then, in the most unexpected situations (like buying an ice cream) God leads us to a prepared heart. Coming from an accounting background, where everything has to fit into its right slot, I tended to be quite rigid in my schedule.

Wednesday was for teaching
Sunday was for preaching (with lots of preparation during the week)
Saturday was for evangelism (with the youth group)
Monday — Whew! At last, a day off!

Spain is known for its spontaneity. People will often react coldly when approached formally about the gospel, but in the middle of a normal conversation it's not unusual for them to pour their hearts out and be open for ministry. Jesus was spontaneous too. (I'm sure that Zacchaeus and the woman at the well would agree.) I thank God that He is using Spain to make me more like Jesus! For me that may mean being prepared to pray with an alcoholic or drug addict late at night, to preach a sermon at ten minutes' notice, or to share the gospel in the hot sun while an ice cream melts in my hand.

Failing

It was time for the meeting in Nazaret to start. I felt depressed as I looked around the room at the four or five faithfuls, thinking of all those who should have been there. "Not many here, are there?" said the pastor to whom I was responsible.

Nazaret is a low-class, port-side suburb of Spain's third largest city, Valencia. During the present century at least four attempts to plant a church there have failed. A year beforehand, the situation seemed to be changing. Gordon McLean (WEC New Zealand) began teaching a small group of women and one old man in the local park. Suddenly the group began to grow and, when Gordon was called back to New Zealand, a group of twenty were rejoicing together in the Lord.

I had then been given the responsibility of leading the group and seeing a church established in the area. (At that time we were collaborating with a nearby Baptist church.) We had found a hall for the meetings and for a while the blessing had continued. Then all of a sudden everything had begun to fall apart and now, a year later, the vision was fading fast.

As I continued looking around the room, I thought of a day's outreach we had had with a group from the Operation Mobilisation ship *Logos* when it was visiting Valencia. The hall had been full of locals from Nazaret; the Lord's presence had seemed very real, and there had been great interest in the message. I had made a brief exit to drive the *Logos* folk back to their ship, while the rest remained for a cup of tea. When I returned, the atmosphere in the hall had changed dramatically. People were walking out with scowls on their faces, some declaring, "I'm not going back to *that* place!" Subsequent investigations revealed that two of the key local women had begun an argument which led to a furious debate, destroying the spirit of love which had previously prevailed.

Then I thought of Miguel, the violent alcoholic. At times we had spent nearly every night of the week counselling and praying for him. His continual ups and downs during several months had drawn heavily on our strength. At last we thought that he had finally been delivered from both alcohol and violence. He seemed so changed. Then suddenly he turned his back on us, having told his children that he was committing his life to Satan. He had then set about deliberately trying to destroy the church by spreading false rumours throughout the community.

There had been many such disappointments.

"Not many here, are there?" Perhaps that was just an innocent comment from the pastor's point of view, but it sowed seeds of hurt in my soul which remained for the succeeding months before we went on furlough. The church decided to abandon attempts to establish a work in Nazaret, and to me those few words said, "You've been a failure." And the worst of it was that it was true! I could give a list of twenty reasons why the work didn't prosper — all good ones. Spain is a hard country. But in the end I was responsible and I had failed.

Learning

Although we had experienced some encouragement in another suburb of Valencia, I returned to New Zealand in 1984 crushed in spirit, doubting if I could ever really be used by God.

Furlough for me was a time of overhaul; sins had to be dealt with and a caring pastor prayed for healing and deliverance in various areas of my life. As I received ministry in the presence of the Lord, I began to discover things about myself that I had never seen before. I saw that rather than being concerned about the failure of the work in Nazaret I was more worried about *my* failure as a person. I realised that I was looking for success in my ministry in order to be acceptable to myself and to other people. I was covering up a sense of insecurity which had been there all my life but which I had tried to hide. After all, who wants to admit that he is insecure?

God in His grace accepts us and uses us as we are, not when we try to be something else by human effort. Paul said that God's grace was sufficient for him, because God's power was made perfect in his weakness (2 Corinthians 12:9). But I had not been prepared to face up to my weaknesses and admit my need. Does God have to put us through such drastic measures to teach us things that seem so simple? In my case the answer was 'yes'.

Proving

The story has a positive ending. The Spirit of God has made this 'strength made perfect in weakness' principle real to my heart. I don't worry about insecurity any more. I know that I'm weak and I rejoice in my weaknesses (my heart is bubbling over as I write this), because God is my strength. I don't have to be capable of achieving anything because God in me is perfectly able.

After furlough we moved to Madrid, and a few months ago I was appointed leader of a small team of missionaries, with the aim of planting a church in the middle-class suburb of Concepción. In some ways Concepción is like Nazaret: a hard area; other attempts have failed; few contacts. What is different is my attitude. I have not come to this work trying to muster up my strengths. I have come rejoicing in my weaknesses. Our team here know some of them, and no doubt in the future they will discover others! I've given up expecting anything from myself, but I'm expecting much from "... Him who is able to do immeasurably more than all we ask or imagine, according to *His* power that is at work within us."

Points to Ponder:
1. Is your daily programme flexible enough for you to make time for people?
2. In your service for God are you demonstrating your ability, or God's power in your weakness?

Relevant scriptures:
1. John 4:4-14.
2. 2 Corinthians 4:7-12, 2 Corinthians 12:9-10.

3

MY CULTURE — OR HIS KINGDOM?

Paul Finch

Unexpected trauma

I thought the words 'culture shock' were history for me. After all, what could be worse than the nine months I had just lived through in Italy? Who would have thought that a shy London-born bank clerk would end up sticking a pin through the shell of a raw egg, and sucking it for his breakfast? Could anything be more traumatic than to discover that the modern house in which you are a guest has no bathroom facilities at all, and that you simply have to roam the countryside for a quiet spot? Besides, I reasoned, hadn't I been brought totally to the end of my Britishness as I lay feverishly in bed in a southern Italian home, my eyes and skin deep yellow with jaundice, and my brain totally out of control? Hadn't God taught me to live through culture shock? Surely He had! Now, as I faced going to seminary in the United States, I would have no problems with a cultural transition at all.

I was wrong. The first few weeks in the USA were fascinating, scintillating, and I was the centre of attraction. I was guest speaker at women's meetings, banquets and seminars. I was elected to the seminary student committee as 'missions representative'. What other groups could boast a foreign speaker and delegate? My British accent was a sure winner. All I had to do, I was told, was to speak about the weather in clear British melodic tones, and dozens would respond to my altar call. Unfortunately, as the novelty wore off, and the 'Paul, the British missionary to Italy' fascination died, a grey loneliness set in. The students around me watched with raucous laughter the various TV programmes. To me they were quite stupid. American football was outrageously violent and nonsensical to one who had enjoyed British football, and had played for the school that superb game of finesse and skill called rugby. The myriad snack foods, the monster cars, the casual use of language, the carefree attitude of so many, all contrasted radically with my conservative European heritage, and I felt alone, very much alone.

Every night I spent hours crying and walking through the nearby park. I was twenty-one years old, and had been so successful in my short three-and-a-half-year career with Lloyds Bank. Now I was tragically unsuccessful! I did not understand Americans. They certainly did not understand me. What was worse, they didn't even care. I will probably never forget those traumatic days, weeks and months.

Twenty years on, I now realise the awesome depths of those two words 'culture shock'. I had thought my struggles in Italy had well prepared me for life in the USA, but had totally underestimated the complexity of this phenomenon. I can see now that, to a greater or lesser extent, shock is really part of every transition of life, one way or another.

In 1971, seven years after those lonely American days, I found myself again in despair.

This time I was in Austria at an International Training Course, and was bitterly disturbed at my nonacceptance by the various national groupings. To all the British participants I was clearly American; to all the Americans I was obviously British; to the Italians, it didn't matter whether I was British or American, I was totally foreign. Well, who was I? I simply did not know. The more I tried to be American, or British, or Italian, the more I knew that I didn't fit anywhere. I was lost. I was a twenty-eight-year-old missionary to Italy who didn't know who he was, and who didn't know which way to go. I was born in England, my wife was American, I was living in Italy, and we had a baby daughter! What was she? American, English or Italian?

Then, in my extreme desolation, God met me. He began to show me what was 'me' and what was 'culture'.

My culture, and me

In any situation of transition there are three essential components, two of them objective and the third subjective. The two objective factors are the two different worlds, and between these the subjective factor, the person moving from one to the other. There is the old world, which is familiar, where customs, values and behaviour patterns have all been subconsciously absorbed and are ingrained as 'normal'. There is the new world with which we are unfamiliar, which has unknown customs and life patterns. Lastly there is a 'me' or a 'you' moving between the two. If I were to sketch it, it would look something like this:

As I moved from the old to the new, from England to America for example, I always used two coping mechanisms. I either tried to use the old life-patterns in the new, or else I looked for the old in the new. But neither of these tricks works. In America I was invited to a friend's house where I was offered strawberry pie and cream. Typical to my English background I graciously declined, fully expecting to be asked again in a more insistent manner. Unfortunately, the hostess, typical to her American background, took my first answer to be the genuine one, and there I sat, alone, looking at all the folk eating delicious pie and cream. My old life pattern had failed me in the new world. On the other hand, in autumn 1969, when we came to a restless and agitated Italy, we searched everywhere for popcorn, pancake mixes, and English breakfast cereal. They just weren't there! You don't find the old in the new.

The two worlds, or cultures, were separate and different, and what I see now, and didn't then, is that every transition we make involves some sort of inner disturbance. Going to a new shop, moving to a new home, a new office, or a new school, all produce a fluttering feeling in our stomachs as we ask ourselves, "Where do I have to go?" "What will my new neighbours be like?" "What will my teachers be like?" It is a new world, and coming from the old one we don't know what to expect. We feel uncertain about ourselves and develop subtle mechanisms in an attempt to reassure ourselves.

God, my environment

Back in 1971, in Austria, God began to teach me a very important lesson: personal identity is not dependent on environment. It is for most people. That's why it is hard to switch worlds. But it is different for the Christian. He has an identity which goes far deeper than culture. He is known to God personally, by name. He is a son or a daughter. He belongs to a royal family. Suddenly, there in Austria, in my 'dark prison', light began to dawn. I began to see how Abraham, for example, could live without all the known cultural supports. He belonged to God, and knew God would support him no matter in which world he lived or moved. I saw how the apostle Paul could lay down all his 'Jewishness', letting it be considered rubbish, simply because he knew he belonged to God. When called a traitor and a heretic, he stood unmoved, knowing that only by the grace of God he was who he was. Finally I came to see how I can be a total mixture of cultures, English, American and Italian, and it doesn't matter, because I am a son, one of God's royal family.

Repeatedly, with my wife Elaine, and my daughters Cristina and Loretta, I am called to cross cultures. Most of 1985 was lived in Italy, but we spent the Christmas holidays in England, and three-and-a-half months in the USA. Constantly, as we make these trips, there is a sense of being ill at ease. We are not always sure how to act in some circumstances. At times we feel totally out of place. The wonderful thing is that it does not matter any more. This summer I made several mistakes. I constantly barged through doors ahead of the ladies, and I'm always reaching for people's hands wanting to greet every Anglo-Saxon as though he were a demonstrative Italian. But when the other person stares back at me, and quizzically puts his hand back into his pocket, I don't feel shunned and ashamed; I quickly understand that I didn't act correctly according to his cultural pattern. But that fact does not threaten my identity any more. I'm privileged to belong to an unchanging God and, although my life is given to working out proper ways of relating to people in various cultures, I also know that God has given me an unchanging identity — Paul Finch, His son.

Point to Ponder:
1. Does your security depend on *where* you are, or *who* you are?
2. The certainty of the known is usually easier to accept than the uncertainty of the unknown. Yet does not spiritual progress come through proving God in new ways and circumstances?

Relevant scriptures:
1. Philippians 4:11-13, Acts 18:9-11.
2. Hebrews 11:1-8, Psalm 56:3-4.

4

MY GOOD SELF — OR JESUS ONLY?

Hester Withey

In Chinese Tibet

"What!" I exclaimed. "How can 'good' be 'bad'?"

I was a missionary in 'Chinese Tibet' at the time. Being what is known as an 'MK', with missionary parents and grandparents on both sides of the family, I had rather taken for granted this business of being a missionary.

WEC had five workers in Chinese Tibet, the name given to the area in eastern Tibet which was, in 1947, under the old Chiang Kai Shek regime of China. They ruled it politically up to the Yangtze river (which flows north/south at that point), and allowed foreigners to live there. In every other respect the area was Tibetan: the majority of the population, the transport (no wheels at all), food, culture, coinage. Both Chinese and Tibetan were spoken. The phrase "a missionary to Tibet" usually referred, in those days, to one working in that particular area. It was more than an alien border situation, but it was not Tibet proper, under the Dalai Lamas. Apart from some Roman Catholic monks who had a monastery between 1725 and 1745, Tibet has never had a resident missionary in the history of the world. Visitors have gone, such as the well-known Sadhu Sundar Singh, but no one has been allowed to stay there to share Jesus with the people.

We five workers were trying to be the 'daring-all-for-Jesus' types that we had been taught to be. But something else had crept in too: "We'll get through to Tibet proper! We'll show these other missionaries, who have been camping on the borders all these years, that it can be done! We'll show 'em! Forward march! We'll throw our lives away for Jesus! We're not 'chocolate soldiers'!"

The plan was to proceed to a new area nearer to the border of Tibet proper. This town of Kantse had never had any Christian residents. We would seek to open up a new work, using a medical clinic as our approach to the people. It was all very primitive and rugged, and travel was extra dangerous because of bandits in the area.

The fly in the ointment — me!

The only real problem for me was that I could not get along with one of my co-workers. Everything she did annoyed me! Yet I had to recognise that she was the one that God used to bring people through to a new or a more vital relationship with Himself, whether they were raw heathen, nominal Christians, missionaries, or WEC staff members. It did not matter whether she spoke to them in English or Mandarin, God used her mightily.

But for me, things would go along peacefully for just so long. Then I would explode, trying to change Margaret or put her straight. Of course, afterwards there were tears, repentance, and pleas for forgiveness. I knew the value of the Bible teaching on 'walking in the light' (1 John 1:7), but the same problem would keep building up in me. I hated myself. I couldn't blame the others. My reactions were the problem. I even thought of leaving the field, but I knew I would only take myself with me wherever I went.

At home there had been inspiring Christian meetings, which had been like spiritual props. Back there I had gathered the impression I was somewhat spiritual. But here, stripped of all that, there didn't seem to be much spirituality left. The climax came one day when the field leader called me for a chat. "Hester," he began, "we want to send a team to Dege (a town between Kantse and the Tibetan border). This will be our next advance. We feel it best that Edith and Margaret go, and that you stay here in Kangting with my wife who, as you know, is pregnant. I have to go away for a month or two on business, but will be back as soon as I can. It wouldn't be advisable for you, or good for the work, if you went into the new territory, because of this relationship problem."

I went to my room alone. "So this is it!" I meditated. "I, who was going to do such big things with God in Tibet, am held back not by mountains, rigorous climate, bandits, nor even lack of government permits, but by *myself*! I'm a liability to God, not an asset!"

The Dege trip never did take place, but God did a wonderful work in Kantse among Chinese while Margaret and Edith were up there alone. Later I went up to join them along with another worker who had just come out.

Then, in keeping with His sense of humour, God used Margaret to help me. She came to me one day, "Hester, I know what your trouble is." I felt furious inside, "If so, why didn't she tell me long ago! I know, she'll just mouth platitudes that I could say myself!" But the Holy Spirit reminded me, "Didn't you tell the others that you'd listen if any of them had any advice for you? Now face up to your promise!" So I went out to the back yard with Margaret, all bundled up in winter clothing, to talk. As soon as she began, I knew every word was from God. "You have been examining yourself, looking for some root of evil that causes your reactions. But you dealt with those in your previous experiences with God. Your problem now is your 'good self'."

"What!" I exclaimed, "How can 'good' be 'bad'?"

"Well," she said, "you have natural strong qualities, and you have been working from your natural humanity — that nature which was tainted at the Fall. You've been functioning from what the Bible calls 'the flesh', meaning that old nature. God can't use that for His purposes. Only what is born of God's Spirit is of any use to God. He has been showing you this, and the difference between the two."

I saw she was right. God illuminated it to my spirit. She went on, "Jesus died on the cross for this nature also, for Romans 6 tells us that we were included with all our enemies, inner and outer, in the death of Jesus. He dealt with them all to set us free. He didn't deal just with our sins but with our basic fallen nature, and all our other enemies. You must die to all of your old self and its ways and preferences. Let the Lord put it all to death as you give it to Him. No one can crucify himself. But you and I *were* crucified with Him — potentially — .2000 years ago. Believe it, give up, surrender, and receive all He did for us. All that is useful to God is His Son, ministered in us and through us, by the Holy Spirit. Die to all else."

As instructed by Margaret, I wrote out all the

aspects of the 'good self' as well as those of the 'bad self' and then across the lot I scribbled the words of Galatians 2:20, "I am crucified with Christ." It was a cold-blooded transaction with God, with no emotion beyond the original desolation and repentance. But I knew it was God's time. He meant business with me, and I certainly meant business with Him. We agreed together about it! I knew I had to believe that God would do His part. My part was to cease from struggling, and believe what He had already done, identifying with it.

Jesus in me

How did it work out?

The next morning at the breakfast table Edith presented me with a drawing of a tombstone, mounted over a nice grassy mound. On the stone was written, "Hester died . . .", and the previous day's date. I kept that to present to the devil in case he forgot I really had died!

It wasn't long before he tried to make me forget. Margaret did something I didn't like, and the old feelings began to come to the surface. Not trusting myself to stay with Margaret, I fled to my room and, on my knees, began to mumble Colossians 3:3, "I am dead and my life is hid with Christ in God." I meant business, and so did God. "I don't have to behave like this any more. That old nature is not me!" I cried. Suddenly, as though a balloon had been pricked, all the horrible feelings evaporated. I knew I loved Margaret again — which, after all, was what I really felt for her. I hadn't wished her ill, only that she would improve! What a relief! Something had really worked. In fact, it worked every time. But if I tried other methods, they didn't work at all.

Not long after, a new awareness began to dawn, so sweet and glorious, "It's really 'Christ in me the hope of glory!' Yes, it really is! He in me can do it all, He really can. Anything necessary to fulfil His will, He can do even in *me*. I just need to get out of the way so He can function."

Looking at it in retrospect, perhaps I should have been able to take such a stand on the power of the work of Jesus on the Cross earlier, and so saved us all such a long, agonizing dying process. But I'm not sure. I needed to be disillusioned with myself and my own energies, and to see how they hindered God. There is no alternative to 'ceasing from our own works' if God is going to do His.

Well, I never did go further into Tibet proper, any more than all those other faithful workers around the border — until 1985. Then I went as a tourist. God is doing a new thing, opening the way for tourists and teachers of English to enter Tibet. There is still no freedom, because it is now a Communist-dominated country. But more is possible now than ever before in its history. God has His time clock. He has not forgotten His people hidden behind the Himalayas, behind the darkness of Buddhist temples and demonic powers. God will have the last word.

Points to Ponder:
1. Is your 'good' self getting in the way of God's work?
2. Have you ever, by a definite act of faith, taken your place with Christ on His cross?

Relevant scriptures:
1. Acts 7:20-34.
2. Galatians 2:20, Romans 6:1-14.

5

MY UNDERSTANDING —
OR HIS REVELATION?

Sheila Kilkenny

A vision of progress

It was dark in the room in which I seemed to be standing because the curtains were closed. Suddenly they drew back a little and some light entered. I moved around in the area that I could now see. It was beautifully furnished. Then the curtains drew back further, and I saw other objects for my comfort and needs. Gradually the curtains were drawn right back, and with the increasing light I was able to enjoy more and more of the room.

The vision faded and I realised that God's Spirit had shown me the importance of His work of revelation in my heart. Each revelation enabled me to move further into His provision.

I was on holiday at the WEC Conference Centre in Scotland when the Spirit first showed me that He lived in me. The very day of my arrival God spoke and said that He wanted me to give up my office job, sell my belongings and serve Him abroad. I had two weeks in which to absorb this thought before going home. During that time the Holy Spirit introduced Himself to me through the morning Bible readings. It was as if He said to me, "I live here. I've been inside you since you first responded to Christ." I was delighted, almost delirious, and knew that life would never be the same again. I am so grateful to God that right from the start I knew that He, living in me, would do the work.

I was so sure that God had spoken to me that I lost no time in applying to the WEC Missionary Training College in Glasgow. When I heard that I was accepted I gave in my notice at work, distributed my few personal belongings, and with great joy set off on the first stage of full-time Christian service.

I found some aspects of the training programme very difficult. I, a member of a Brethren Assembly, was expected to take part in public prayer, preach in churches and on street corners! I had never been in a public house, despite coming from a non-Christian home, but on my first Saturday at college I joined a group of women students who went to thirteen public houses to sell *Challenge* magazine. I was very fearful but thanked God that His Spirit was in me to do the work.

Learning to love

After college I went to WEC headquarters in London as a candidate for Senegal, West Africa. I was hungry to know more of the Spirit in my life. I had proved that He, in me, would do the work. But I wanted to know His love in my heart. I did not know how to get it. One day, in desperation, I knelt by my bed and opened the Bible to Luke 11:11-13. I read that my heavenly Father promises to give the Spirit to His children if they ask. So I said, "Would you please fill me with Your Spirit of love?" As I saw no reason to doubt that God would keep His promise, I said "Thank you", rose from my knees and went my way. By evening the peace that had come into my heart had turned to over-flowing joy, and I had a breath-taking realisation of God's great love. I wanted to shout, "God loves me! He loves *me!*"

But some time after that, I was on my knees bewailing the fact that there was someone I couldn't stand. "I don't love her!" I said, thumping the bed. "Help me!" In my heart I heard the words, "I love her." I knew God had spoken. He, the One who loves, lives in me. What a relief! I immediately rejected the thought that the person was un-lovable and embraced the truth that God was crazy about her, that I am joined to Him, and that means that I would find her lovable too. I did.

Released from bondage

But the Christian life has to do with more than working and loving. It has also to do with fighting. After four and a half years among the animistic Jolas in Senegal I came home for a year of rest, punctuated by meetings. I published far and wide the truth that the Jolas are bound by evil spirits. I described their animistic practices. I declared that God had promised to break through and deliver the Jolas, and urged people to pray against Satan in the Name of Jesus.

As I stirred up trouble for Satan, he stirred up trouble for me. I became increasingly depressed. Life ceased to be worth living. My mind was filled with despairing thoughts and I finally decided to commit suicide. I did not know why I was so unhappy. But even in the darkness I cried to God to save me. He heard my prayer and sent two senior WEC missionaries to show me that just as the Jolas needed release from Satan's power, so did I. It had not occurred to me that there was anything occult in my life that called for repentance. But as I prayed with them, the Spirit drew back the curtain of another room, that of my childhood. I saw myself seated at a table with my relations calling on the spirits. As other scenes came to mind, I saw that in ignorance I had been involved in occult activities. But God no longer overlooks such ignorance (Acts 17:30). There and then I renounced the occult and asked for freedom and forgiveness. The depression lifted and life became good again.

Further deliverances

After further years in Senegal, the Spirit shed more light in my heart. I discovered that Satan was binding my mind with fiction. It was my own fault. I have always been an avid reader, and read fiction for relaxation. One day the Lord told me He did not want me to read it any more. I protested vigorously! There were so many things that separated me from non-Christian friends; surely I could be allowed to have one thing in common with them? Besides, I like fiction!

In answer God told me that if I cut out fiction, I would "enter into life". I had chosen to immerse myself in fiction, and now I could control it only with extreme difficulty. The Lord led me to repentance and I cried for help. I asked some friends to pray for me, confessing I had disobeyed the Lord. After I had prayed with them I saw in my mind a long corridor, its walls lined with shelves of books. Then the Lord walked along, taking the books down and throwing them away.

From that moment my mind was clear and receptive once again to the Holy Spirit.

One day I realised that the Spirit of God was not the only spirit expressing itself through me. I was horrified and ashamed. I asked God to confirm this to me, and three times in one day I heard myself uttering unkind words that were not my own and were most certainly not from the Spirit of God. Distressed, I talked to God about it. He showed me that intolerance was a longstanding fault in my character, and that Satan had entered at that point. I asked God to forgive me. In the Name of Jesus I told Satan to take his intolerance out of my life. I found relief. I discovered that situations which would have previously made me angry or impatient no longer did so. It was good to be alerted to the fact that Satan could be illegally squatting in territory that rightly belongs to God.

During a period of six months the Holy Spirit showed me where Satan was expressing himself through me. For years I had been troubled by what I thought of as my own sexuality. It was as if there was a wild animal inside me wanting to break out. I had such trouble keeping it under control. I was afraid that people would discover what I was really like inside. Then one day I discovered that this 'wild animal' was in fact one of Satan's emissaries. I was horrified. Unable to free myself, I went to someone for help. With support, and in the Lord's Name, I disinherited myself from the unclean spirit that had come to me through my family and ordered it to go. Immediately I knew myself to be free and clean. There was no longer anything to be ashamed of. Since that day I have enjoyed being a woman.

I also found to my astonishment that I was bound by fear. I had not considered myself to be fearful, but the Lord made me aware that dread would fill my heart from time to time, especially after I had performed some service for Him: I was afraid of failure. I felt pain in my stomach when I had prayed an audacious prayer; I was afraid of what people would think. He drew my attention to the way I would avoid people who had the gift of discernment; I was afraid of exposure. He showed me all these fears were of Satan. What a relief! How marvellous to know that I could be free of them and enjoy the peace that Jesus died to give me.

With Satan's influence gone from body, mind and emotions, I enjoy serving God more than ever. I can talk freely to people, pray freely with them, stand up in front of a crowd and not feel sick with fear. No words can describe the joy of being able to stand in God's presence without wanting to hide. I realise now that it was Satan who shrank from God's holy presence, but I was so bound by him that I thought the problem was mine.

Living in Christ

The more I have weeded Satan's influence out of my heart, the more I have discovered who I really am. The Biblical statements about me have become excitingly real. I am a new creature. I died with Christ and am living in union with Him. I have a spirit of love, not fear. I am at peace.

Knowing who I am has helped me to identify Satan. I always used to think that every thought that came into my head was mine. I had been taught not to put too much blame on Satan, because it was probably my old, sinful nature coming into operation. But Paul says that those who belong to Christ have crucified the sinful nature (Gal 5:24). So I ceased to believe that the unclean or critical thoughts that came into my mind came from my own spirit. Now I blame Satan and tell him to go away. This new life style has brought great joy and peace; it is what Christ died for. Now I offer my body to God for Him to live His life out through me.

A short while ago the Spirit drew back the curtain a bit more. In a meeting at WEC headquarters we were standing worshipping God, thinking how majestic, high and holy He is. Suddenly my heart began to burn with joy and recognition, "That's my Dad! There is Jesus, my Brother!" Oh joy! I knew that although my Father is indeed the one and only God, surrounded by glorious beings, I can rush up to Him and scramble, as it were, on His knee and have His attention. I can pour out my heart to Him because of our warm, intimate relationship: a trusting child with a loving father.

I am sure that there is a lot more that the Holy Spirit will show me as the years go by. It seems as if He waits for me to move freely in each new area before showing me another truth. I have spent long periods of my life wasting the light that has been shed. At the moment I am busy exploring every corner that I can see, and look forward to the day when I shall know as I am known: completely!

Points to Ponder:
1. Are there things in your life which you have considered to be personal traits, but which are really Satan's emissaries?

2. Does God show us new truths before we have acted on what He has already shown us?

Relevant scriptures:
1. Romans 7:20-25.
2. John 2: 31-32.

SECTION 2

SAVED FROM

STERILE RELIGION

6

A CHRISTIAN LOOK-ALIKE

Andy Lawrance

The 'perfect baby' grows up

My mother said I was a perfect baby. I didn't cry. I slept day and night. I ate all that she fed me. One day I was taken for a routine check-up, and the nurse said I was dying of anaemia. It appeared that I was everything a perfect baby should be, but the examination revealed that I didn't even have enough strength to cry or stay awake.

At times I thought I was a perfect Christian. I didn't complain. I didn't rock the church boat, and I always backed the pastor with my "Amen" whatever his views. I had the appearance of a perfect Christian, but there was a problem. I didn't know God like I should. I didn't have enough of His strength or power.

My father, a deacon in the local church, had died when I was seven, and my first reaction had been, "Well, I won't get any more spankings!" I remember someone giving me a coin at the funeral parlour and that made my day. During the funeral service I started crying like a baby, causing everyone in the little Baptist church to follow suit. However, I didn't get any more money. But I didn't get any more spankings either, not because I didn't deserve them, but simply because I could outrun my mother.

At thirteen I felt the call of God for missionary

service while attending the People's Church
Missionary Conference in Toronto, Canada. I can
remember standing when the appeal was given.
There was just one problem: I wasn't a Christian.

The following year I requested baptism even
though I knew I wasn't saved. I was tired of everyone buttonholing me about salvation, so I testified
to the church about my calling and was baptised. I
went into the water a dry sinner and came out a
wet one. Six months later proved I hadn't
changed, and to my mother's grief I didn't go near
the church. For the next couple of years I was
involved with a local gang and even fought my
way to being leader. At seventeen I practically
forced my mother into signing papers so that I
could join the Canadian Navy.

All at sea — but being prepared

All the spankings I missed while growing up
were stored up as 'kit issue' in the Navy, once I
donned the blue uniform. God had His way of
showing me the value of obedience and the
necessity of discipline. Nor had He forgotten my
former commitment for missionary service. He
was preparing me, and his rod was sometimes
heavy. I'll never forget running with a rifle for a
couple of hours, every day for a week. It makes
your shoulder raw after the first day. Sometimes I
was confined to cells picking hemp. Then there
was the immovable fact of having a five-year con-
tract from which there was no escape. On the
other hand, I spent four of my five years at sea and
proved the truth of God's Word that 'they that go
down to sea in ships see the wonders of God'.

Six months after leaving the Navy I was alone in
my room and God spoke to me through the verse,

Romans 10:9. I needed to 'confess Christ with my mouth'. Immediately I knocked on my mother's bedroom door and told her I was saved. She told me later that she had a praise meeting all night.

The new creature grows up

God delivered me from alcohol, a dirty mouth and all the trash that goes with it. After I came to the Lord I never received another call to missionary service. My previous commitment ten years before was simply confirmed.

A year later Sylvia and I were married and together attended Toronto Bible College. From there we joined WEC and headed off to Brazil in 1962.

On board ship with our two small children (Cindy, aged two, and Wesley, eleven months) we had the use of two cabins, so I used the spare one for seeking the Lord. God spoke to me on that trip and asked, "Andy, why are you going to Brazil?" I answered energetically, "To evangelise Brazilians, establish churches, hold campaigns and whatever else is needed." God's reply was, "No, you are going there to *get to know Me.*" But it was a slow process.

God's menu in Brazil — humble pie

One Sunday I was sure God wanted to revolutionise the interior of the town where we were missionaries. With the eye of faith I could already see Jonas, the crippled street cleaner, leaping higher and shouting louder than the temple cripple. I couldn't wait until the evening service to make the appeal for the lame and sick, because I was sure that God was going to heal them. Sure enough Jonas waddled forward when I gave the invitation. So that one person would not get the glory, the deacons were called forward to support me. Jonas was commanded to jump. He barely budged. "Let's pray again!" He budged the same way. "Let's pray the third time!" We cleared out all the demons of unbelief and Jonas was commanded to jump. This time the budge was hardly noticeable. The pastor looked a fool. God did not answer prayer my way.

Humble pie is God's menu at times. He is not our personal waiter. He is God and He is unique. God is greater than the witness in our hearts or our faith, courage or doctrine. He is God. The question came back to my mind, "Andy, do you really know God?"

God overturns my order of things

One afternoon in that same little town a young girl came running up, pleading with me to pray for her father. He was really sick and hadn't been to work for two days. My first thought was that this man needed to be saved. He had visited our congregation a couple of times and knew the way of salvation but just didn't want to pay the price. "He doesn't deserve to be healed until he's made a decision for the Lord," I thought. "If I were God I would let him suffer a little more for his sin."

Soon, along with one of the deacons and Dave Townshend, my fellow worker from New Zealand, I was on my way to his house. It was a dingy little shack. We were led into an inner room where I could see a light bulb hanging from the ceiling, but it was turned off. Perhaps last month's bill hadn't been paid. The wooden shutters were closed, and as my eyes became accustomed to the darkness I could see a man lying face down on a bed, covered by a sheet. He wasn't dead because he was groaning. He turned on his side and told us about his pain. It was his liver and it was the worst attack he'd ever had. Would we pray for him, was his plea; he was sure he was about to die. I assured him that God does heal, but that his priority was to attend to his soul's need.

For the next five minutes I laid into him, telling him how terrible sin is (especially his) and that Jesus is the only Saviour. All of a sudden he sat up, then stood up, then started shouting, "I'm healed, I'm healed!" I finally calmed him down and told him we hadn't prayed for him yet! I must admit that he took the punch out of my evangelistic sermon and I can't remember if he prayed the sinner's prayer or not, but we prayed and quickly left because he wanted to get to the company and work his shift for the day.

He gave his testimony at church that same week. The question still lingered with me, "Andy, do you really know God and understand His ways?"

Points to Ponder:
1. 'Humble pie — God's menu.' Why does God often allow us to be taken down a peg or two?
2. What is the secret of answered prayer?

Relevant scriptures:
1. Proverbs 16:18, John 2:16, Colossians 3:12-14.
2. Luke 11:1-13, John 16:23-24.

7

FROM TRAINING NOVITIATES TO PLANTING CHURCHES

Graciela Snelling

Trying versus trusting

Having spent nearly ten years in a Colombian convent doing my best to live out my monastic vows of poverty, chastity and obedience, I knew very well what it was to be religious in the fullest sense of that word. In fact, religiosity became ingrained in my character. Later I left the convent and started attending an evangelical church in Bogota, though it took two years for me to really understand that the Christian life is not a question of being religious, but of having a life-transforming relationship with Jesus Christ. God taught me that being a Christian has nothing to do with ceremonies, traditions and formal church-going, but everything to do with maintaining a vital, day-by-day relationship with the Lord Jesus Christ.

At this time, two pastors exercised a great influence upon me, God using them to help mould my Christian character. One of them, Hector Pardo, who was later to become president of the Evangelical Confederation of Colombia, was pastor of the church I attended for almost two years. What impressed me most about him was his complete emotional stability and his refusal to be ruffled by any problem. On one occasion I went with him to a church where he had been invited to preach and where he was also planning to show a film. Before he went, he had great difficulty obtaining a new bulb for the projector. He searched all over the city for several days until at last he found one just a few minutes before the scheduled showing of the film. He handed me the bulb and asked me to carry it to the church, but on arrival it was found to be smashed to pieces inside the box. Hector, instead of becoming angry, frustrated or even embarrassed, reacted with such complete composure and calm that I simply had to marvel at the control which the Holy Spirit obviously had upon his inner life.

The other man, Colin Crawford, a Scotsman, was pastor of the church in which I later became a deaconess. He was a man of tremendous zeal for the Lord and seemed to get through an immense amount of work every day, including preaching, studying, writing, counselling and radio programmes.

His overwhelming passion to see people saved, and his very clear, authoritative presentation of the gospel meant that the church, which he himself had founded a year or so before I joined, grew very rapidly. Now, just twelve years later, it has an attendance of nearly two thousand people on Sunday mornings. His zeal is contagious and helped me to dedicate my life to full-time Christian ministry.

For a while I worked as Colin's secretary and spent long hours typing out the manuscript for a small study book on Paul's letter to the Philippians. As a result, this letter has become very precious to me and its message has made a great impact on my thinking, particularly the clear teaching that we can be useful instruments in God's hands, and experience fullness of joy no matter what our outward circumstances.

The growth of the church during the three years leading up to my marriage at the end of 1977 taught me that, in spite of the experience of many smaller churches which do not seem to grow, it is the will of God that His church should increase and have a strong, authoritative voice in the world. Stagnation is never God's will.

Whilst I was in the convent, the Lord worked in the lives of my mother and my sisters, bringing them to a living faith in Christ. One of my sisters, Floralba, had a testimony which helped me. She was left a widow at twenty-four, with three small children. She had little prospect of remarrying, as very few Colombian men would think of marrying a woman with three children! However, Floralba is a person of great faith and she prayed that the Lord would provide her with a husband and father for her children.

On a visit to Quito, Ecuador, at a Christian convention, she met Dennis, a young US airman who had been praying about a wife. Having been told by the doctors that he could never have children of his own, he was looking for a young Christian woman with a ready-made family! They fell in love and later married.

But, the biggest miracle was still to come. The Lord later gave them another child, in spite of Dennis's supposed sterility, thus making their joy complete. They now have two boys and two girls. Their story was a great stimulus to my own faith when I married the man of God's choice some two years later. Doctors had told me that I could never have children, but He has given us two beautiful daughters, and an exciting ministry of church planting.

Church planting with WEC

My husband, Michael, was already working in the city of Ibague when we married and we spent two more years there working in a very testing situation. The fellowship consisted of about thirty people who had been paying rent for a long while for an unpleasant, poorly-situated meeting room. They had little vision to expand, much less buy a property of their own.

As a couple we pledged before the Lord to look for a suitable plot of ground for the church, and to trust that the fellowship would have their own property before we left. We looked all over Ibague until we finally told the Lord we were tired of searching for a site which did not seem to exist. At this point we simply told the Lord that we would not look any further, but that someone would have to get in touch with us and offer us a suitable plot at a reasonable price.

Within a few days we received a telephone call from a man who offered us a piece of land near to where we were meeting and at a good price! The deal was finalised and the church at last had its own ground. Apart from the down payment of 120,000 Colombian pesos (= £300) which the church had in the bank, we had to pay two instalments of 40,000 pesos (£100) at three-monthly intervals, quite a tall order for a small congregation of poor people. However, in spite of criticism from some members of the congregation, who claimed we were getting the church into debt, we were able to pay the two instalments exactly at the required time.

It was a great lesson in faith for ourselves and the church. It strengthened our conviction that with God all things are possible. After that the church began to grow, and we were able to leave a congregation of about a hundred people at the end of those two years. It now has a regular Sunday attendance of 150 to 160 people.

It was during our time in Ibague that I was able to use the understanding I had acquired of Philippians, to teach a course to the women who met on Wednesday afternoons in our house. Using Colin Crawford's booklet, which I knew almost off by heart, we studied together the great themes of the book and by the end of the study were often melted before the Lord in worship and praise. For several in that small group it was a time of spiritual growth and deepening awareness of the presence and power of God.

After our return from furlough in 1981 we worked for a while in a working-class suburb of Bogotá, but began to feel increasingly that this was not where the Lord wanted us. After much prayer we decided to step out in faith and begin a new work, using our Mission headquarters in the middle-class suburb of Santa Isabel as a base. At the beginning of 1983 we held our first Sunday service in our own living/dining room with ten people present, six of whom were missionaries. Now a group of fifty to sixty people meet on Sunday mornings. God is working in response to the faith of His people. We are trusting Him for a big church which will exert an increasing influence on this large middle-class suburb.

Points to Ponder:
1. Stagnation is never God's will. Is there anything for which you should be trusting God, in order to move forward His work?
2. Is it scriptural to believe that God works not only in individuals but in families?

Relevant scriptures:
1. 2 Corinthians 4:16, 1 John 5:1-5.
2. Acts 16:30-32, Acts 16:14-15.

8

SOUGHT OUT TO BE
A SOUL-WINNER

RAFAEL VEGA

Those dreaded evangelicals

I was born into a Roman Catholic family. My own parents were never married and lived separately, so my father's parents brought me up because I was taken away from my mother when I was very small. They saw to my education, being keen for me to become a school teacher. In Colombia Catholicism is the national religion, so I grew up knowing all the religious rites. I was well instructed in religion, but knew nothing of salvation or peace of heart.

I spent the end of 1958 and the beginning of 1959 on vacation at my grandparents' house in the country. By that time some missionaries were working in the area. Many people became Christians (but not my father's relations who were, and are, steeped in the traditions and teachings of the Roman Catholic Church).

Some believers invited me along to the Sunday meetings in the little church built by the evangelicals. I was afraid to attend, because it was considered a sin according to the teaching I had received in religious classes. So I didn't accept the invitations given by the believers, but God used some of my friends, companions in revelry, who

persuaded me to go to a special 'fiesta' when the
evangelicals were celebrating 'Mother's Day'. The
idea was to watch the celebration, as they called it,
and ignore the rest. My riotous friends' intentions
had nothing to do with seeking God.

Everything was very beautiful at the 'fiesta'.
When the missionary gave God's message, I felt an
inner convicting power speaking to me about my
life. It was something I had never known before.

I join the evangelicals

Other Sundays passed by and I returned to the
meetings, this time on my own account. In May
1959 I surrendered my life to the Lord. What a
wonderful experience, as joy and peace entered
my life! A few days later the relatives in my grandparents' home found out about my decision and
began to give me a hard time. My friends, and the
companions who took me to the meeting house in
the first place, also despised me. But I was so con-
tented that their rejection wasn't important to me.

Shortly after my conversion I had a great urge
to take the gospel message to an uncle (my
mother's brother). I decided to make my first
'missionary' journey to the region where he lived
with his in-laws. I arrived and told them all that
God had done in my life. Both my uncle and his
in-laws accepted the Lord Jesus as their Saviour.

These were the first three souls that I won for
Christ. The longing that my family should know
Christ burned in my heart, and when I gave testimony to my mother, my brothers and other relatives, they also followed the Lord.

So the desire was born in me to serve the Lord
by helping others to find Christ. I was new in the
ways of the Lord, and very inadequately prepared,

but I wanted to serve Him. At the beginning of 1960 someone told me about the WEC Bible Institute in Bogotá, where young people were trained for the ministry, and I felt I ought to go. I was able to take this step of faith, because the brothers had taught me about having faith in the Lord, and not in myself.

I made my application, trusting God to supply the fees for the studies — and so it happened! He supplied my need, and I was accepted. I was not without my problems, but I finished my training there in 1963.

I become a missionary

In 1964 I got married, and my wife, Hermita, and I began serving the Lord full time. For fourteen years we served in our own country, but in 1977 God gave us a new call, to leave Colombia and go to serve Him in Uruguay. It was a very difficult decision, and the Lord had to deal with me, my wife and our five children. The wonderful thing was that He put in all of us the united desire to obey His call.

On 3 October, 1978, at the Dorado Airport in Bogotá, we said goodbye to our Colombian relatives, friends, missionaries and colleagues. We left our inheritance, our country, and our old field of service where the Lord had taught us how to bear difficulties and testings. The next day we landed on Uruguayan soil to begin a new era in our service.

Several years have already passed. The Lord has provided for us and blessed our ministry. My wife and I, together with our five children, form a team to serve the Lord, because God has given musical gifts to our children. To see them helping in the meetings, and serving the Lord by my side, is one of the greatest blessings of my life.

In writing this account I have shed a few tears, because I see how wonderful God is. It is a tremendous joy to testify to the blessing of being where the Lord wants us to be.

Points to Ponder:
1. Are you where the Lord wants you to be, spiritually and geographically?
2. Is it right to have a sense of responsibility for unsaved members of your family? How would God have you to act in this matter?

Relevant scriptures:
1. Romans 12:1-2.
2. John 1:40-42, Mark 5:18-20, John 4:28-29.

9

GOD — WHERE ARE YOU?

Creuza Santana

Where God was not

All through my childhood I saw my parents make frequent visits to a special city in Brazil. There all the devoted Catholics go at least once a year to do many different kinds of penance. They crawled on their knees up the steps to a large church, and then bought candles to burn to the Virgin Mary so that she would intercede for them and help them in their troubles.

I joined with them in all this until I was seventeen. Then a great feeling of dissatisfaction and emptiness came into my life as I realised that religion could not change people. I found myself full of bitterness, telling many lies.

I couldn't find power or reality in the Church, so for one year I tried spiritism. It only made things worse. I had to take a lot of pills because I couldn't sleep. In fact I became so ill that when I was twenty my parents sent me away to a farm for a rest. They thought I was going to die.

One afternoon at the farm I was out riding. Suddenly I stopped the horse, looked up to heaven and shouted, "God, where are You? I need You! Please help me, please speak to me. I want to know You. I can't stand life any more."

At that moment the word 'Bible' came into my mind. Until then I had never read the Bible. I borrowed one that day and started reading it, but I couldn't understand it.

How I found Him

A month later a friend invited me to a Christian church. I was furious, for I hated the very sight of Protestants. I told her that I was born a Catholic and I would die one. She spent the whole night praying that God would bring me back to her house and save me. While I was having a party with my friends she was in battle with the powers of darkness on my behalf!

The next morning nothing and nobody could stop me from going to her house, even though it was in another town. She took me along to her church. It was a Pentecostal one and it made me angry; I couldn't understand how people could talk so freely to a God I could not see.

But at one point the preacher seemed to address himself to me in the middle of almost a thousand people! He spoke about the parable of the lost sheep and I knew that I was that lost sheep. Right then I met the living God. I cried for an hour at His feet. He received me, healed me, and restored my life, which had been in such a mess. He told me then that I was chosen from the womb to be His ambassador.

Called to be an ambassador

For a while I did not understand the signifi-cance of this call, but a few months later, while I was praying, the Lord showed me a name written on a road sign. It was Venice.

Three years later, in my final year at Bible School, He spoke again as I was asking Him about my next step. I had a dream in which a lady I knew came to me and said, "Creuza, get prepared to leave Brazil. You will be sent out by a mission." Later on I phoned her and shared my dream. She took me to a couple who introduced me to WEC in Brazil.

I submitted my application to WEC and was invited to attend the four-month Candidate Course at its headquarters in Belo Horizonte.

I will never forget the day when I stood in line to buy my bus ticket. I had two new leather suitcases by my side, seven people in front of me and others behind. There I was — shut in with God, because I hadn't a cent towards my fare!

I prayed, "Lord, You're sending me, and I'm willing to go but I have no ticket and no money! It's over to You!" The countdown continued . . . seven, six, five, four, three, two passengers in front. Then God stepped in!

"Ah, Creuza, where are you going?" It was an old friend.

"To the WEC headquarters in Belo Horizonte, to do my Candidate Orientation Course. I feel called to serve the Lord in Italy."

"How interesting! I was to go on this bus, but can't. Like to buy my ticket?"

"I certainly would," (but Lord, I don't have any cash!). Drawing the ticket from his pocket and passing it over to me, he said, "Don't worry about the money!"

I left Brazil in 1983, spending almost three years on the OM ships *Doulos* and *Logos*. I have been to Italy, the very place that God showed me 14 years ago. Now I am trusting for a visa to go there permanently.

When I first came to the Lord my family (eight brothers and one sister) almost killed me for deserting their religion. Now half of them are saved too! One thing I know for sure, "Everyone who calls on the name of the Lord will be saved."

The greatest joy of my life is to know the risen Christ. The second is to see others finding Him. These are my aims in life.

Points to Ponder:
1. Do you know how to battle in prayer against the powers of darkness, so that people are released from their control?
2. What is your main aim in life?

Relevant scriptures:
1. Ephesians 6:10-18.
2. Philippians 3:7-14.

SECTION 3

GOD'S SCHOOL

FOR LEADERS

10

STRANGE TURNS ON A DESERT ROAD

Dieter Kuhl

Signpost one: God's Sovereignty

Never would I become a physician! It was torture for me to sit in health lessons at school and to look at those horrible wall charts showing details of the human body. I could not get rid of the feeling of someone stabbing a knife into my knees or cutting my sinews. My interest lay in another field: history. I would become a professor in history.

However, "In his heart a man plans his course, but the Lord determines his steps" (Proverbs 16:9). One day, when I was still in the upper sixth and on my way home from school, suddenly, out of the blue, an assurance entered my heart. Its clarity and content stunned me: "You must become a missionary doctor." I was not even a born-again Christian then. Yes, I went to the local YMCA and had started to read my Bible regularly, but I knew nothing about personal guidance. I had never even thought of missions, yet this assurance was there, sudden and forceful. It became the turning point of my life. Six months later I left for Saarbrücken University to start medical training. But I didn't speak to anyone about the real reason for this step.

· As I recall this event now, over twenty-five years later, I can only say, God's ways are mysterious. In

His sovereignty He picked me out of thousands of my contemporaries, set me on a track totally different from that which I had planned, and said, "I have a special task for you." I accepted it without much thinking and without any struggle. A year later, my YMCA secretary wrote to me, "Last week God told me that you will go to the mission field." I had not told him. Our God is a living and sovereign God.

Signpost two: God's faithfulness

During my second year in university I came to know Jesus as my personal Saviour and Lord. I learned to trust and obey God and to follow Him step by step. I joined the Fellowship of Evangelical Students, and this relationship with other Christians, who also had a burden for world missions, proved crucial in keeping me on track. Almost forty of them went to the mission field and two became leaders of German evangelical missionary societies.

I investigated various medical missions, challenged by the great need. Then the burden for Muslim countries came more and more into focus, till I was sure that it was amongst them that the Lord wanted me to work. But where? One evening the Lord spoke clearly to me in my quiet time through reading Isaiah 66:18-20: "the distant islands . . .". I had heard missionaries from Indonesia say that Christians there applied this expression to their country, an archipelago consisting of over 13,000 islands.

But was it right to take a verse of Scripture and to interpret it in such a personal way? I longed for clarity and assurance, so I asked the Lord to confirm this guidance to Indonesia by speaking to

Renate (my fianceé) in a similar way, without my interference.

Eight months passed before He spoke to Renate in her daily Bible reading about "the islands" (Isaiah 51:5). She struggled for about three weeks because it was so different from what she expected. Nor did she know about 'my' country! What if it was different? Peace came through obedience. "Lord, it is Your responsibility." Then we learned that He had shown both of us, separately and clearly, the same country!

Signpost three: Obedience

After consulting with the German sending base of WEC International, South Sumatra became our target area. It was a remote rural region where in 1964 a small church had come into being. Almost all members of the emerging church had formerly been Muslims. Three simple clinics had been started to provide basic medical treatment. Our vision was to co-ordinate the medical ministry and to train medical auxiliaries to do personal evangelism.

We knew we would need to run a small hospital with facilities for surgery, so we planned further training, which would take another three to four years.

One morning, Acts 8:26ff spoke clearly to my heart, "Go south to the road . . . So he started out." Deep in my heart the Lord seemed to say: "Stop your specialist training now and get ready to leave for Indonesia." For three weeks I struggled. I had my teeth into something which I loved and which I pursued with all my heart, even with spiritual justification. But I knew that if I were disobedient the Lord's peace would leave me. On the very last day possible for handing in my resignation from hospital, I submitted it. The peace never left. We applied for WEC and entered Candidate Course in April 1971.

Signpost four: Willingness to be redirected

We set out for Indonesia in October 1972, looking forward to starting our medical and Bible teaching ministry in the Serawai church. All Central Government Departments, as well as the medical authorities of Bengkulu province, had already given their approval. Everything depended on the approval of the governor of Bengkulu province who had the final say. But he said "No"and his "No" stood firm. We tried again. Had we misinterpreted the will of God? Was God testing our faith? We moved to Bengkulu province without the approval of the governor, as that was not required for staying in the province and working as pastors. Letters from home said, "What a waste! Aren't you on the wrong track?" But the peace of God passes all understanding. It did not even seem a sacrifice to let the medical ministry go and concentrate on a spiritual ministry.

Then the Lord opened another door for us: teaching at the Indonesian Bible Institute in Java, with an emphasis on training rural pastors in health education, community development, and agriculture. We had wanted to equip medical auxiliaries with Bible training. Now we were to train rural pastors in practical subjects. This gave us a much wider impact than by being located in Serawai. When we moved to Java I knew that I would never get back into a medical ministry. It had been God who stopped my specialist course in gynaecology and obstetrics. We moved in peace.

Signpost five: Willing to be made willing

Learning the lesson of obedience and total dependence on Him is not finished in a day. It never finishes. God wants us to be always flexible and alert to His plan, which He makes plain if we are willing to follow wherever He leads.

Our ministry in the Indonesian Bible Institute developed over the years. Besides teaching practical subjects, I became lecturer in Church History. It had been my 'first love' during high school. Now it was God's extra for me.

In 1977 I became academic dean of the college, and in 1980 its vice principal. I was able to finish my B.Th. An MA in missiology followed. The Lord had taken me out of medical work altogether and established me in theological training. We both felt that this teaching ministry was His plan for our future. We loved Indonesia. We loved the rapidly expanding national ministry of the Indonesian Missionary Fellowship. It was His place for us.

By now the visa policy of the Immigration Department was becoming more and more restrictive, but the Indonesian Government started to offer Indonesian citizenship to expatriate missionaries so that they could stay in the country. We investigated this possibility, accepted it wholeheartedly, and started preparations that would lead to an application for Indonesian citizenship.

Returning from furlough in 1982 we travelled to Indonesia via the WEC Headquarters in England. We were shaken to the depths when WEC's International Secretary asked us, "Would you pray about your possible nomination for the position of International Secretary?" We thought it was a joke. When we realised that it was meant seriously, our reaction was, "No, never!" We were going to settle in Indonesia which we loved so much.

The important next step was to be willing to be made willing. We prayed daily that the meeting of WEC leaders in Germany would not be able to agree to our nomination and would be led to nominate someone else. But funnily enough, the more we prayed the more deeply we knew in our hearts that it would happen! Eventually God made us willing to leave what we loved and to lose face with our Indonesian brothers and sisters by telling them of the proposed nomination and of our willingness to be again on the move for Him, wherever He leads.

Points to Ponder:
1. Can you think of things that could be a mental or emotional block against knowing the will of God (e.g. security, career, friendship, desire to please others, slack life style)?
2. Should a fiancée/wife be able to receive guidance directly from the Lord, or should she take her husband's guidance for herself?

Relevant scriptures:
1. Romans 8:14, Mark 10:17-23.
2. 1 Peter 3:1-12, Colossians 3:15, Psalm 32:8-9.

11

THE MISSIONARY 'IMAGE' PUT ME OFF!

Heather Wraight

I'll do it my way

"Mum, I think God wants me to be a missionary, but please don't ever let me look like one!" I was fifteen, and just home from a Crusader (Bible Class) houseparty. In a way this was not a surprise. My Christian parents brought me up to expect that I would be a missionary, but I still had to reach the point of personal conviction about it, just as I had had to make my own decision about being a Christian.

I had recently taken 'O' level examinations. At school I quietly enjoyed the music of The Beatles, but I dare not admit to that at home! Even though we were now attending a Baptist church, our Brethren background still imposed fairly strict rules about things considered 'worldly'. However, in the early sixties young people's attitudes were changing, and as a teenager I found I was not too impressed by some of the missionaries I met.

Fortunately for everyone, I couldn't leave home to go overseas at fifteen. The family did travel though, and for a year we lived in Toronto, Canada, attending a church that was far more missionary-minded than the one back home. The desire to serve God grew, but I intended to do it my way. I trained as a nurse, something I had wanted to do since I was about five. At the end of the three years I considered myself God's gift to any missionary society lucky enough to get hold of me! I planned to go to Africa, as soon as possible, but the first society I approached insisted I attend Bible College. What a bore!

I blustered through the first term at Redcliffe College, with much the same attitude I had to most things: do enough work to get by and enjoy yourself the rest of the time. For me enjoyment was not in studying the Bible, but in making new friends, reading avidly, representing college in sports, and being away from home. Needless to say the staff did not think those were the right reasons for my being there. The vice principal particularly got under my skin. She prayed, counselled me whether I wanted her to or not, and persisted until, after five terms, God got through to me.

Getting down to bedrock

At last I realised that though my Christian background had taught me much, the evidence had to be seen in my life. It was no good telling the children in my Sunday School class that God loves everyone, while I carefully avoided the students I did not like. Breaking the rules, even if I did think some of them were petty, was not acceptable. Obedience is one of the keystones of the Christian life, and I discovered I had a lot to learn.

It brought me up short to realise that my plans were not God's plans. While I was at college I was told it would be medically inadvisable for me to live in a tropical climate, which ruled out Africa. I wondered if God was directing me to something other than nursing. About the same time British

WEC Headquarters moved from South London to about five miles from my home, and lots of what I considered terribly 'holy' missionaries started attending my church. Imagine my surprise when I applied for a course on Christian radio and discovered it was to be held at the WEC headquarters, and run by a group within WEC who worked in Britain. This turned out to be God's plan for me.

Doing it God's way

I went back to nursing for two years before I was accepted by WEC to work with Radio Worldwide. Then I threw myself into radio work. I loved it. My mother writes Christian books, and my father has always had tape recorders around the house, so the two sides of programme production presented no fears. There was so much to learn that I sat in on every recording session, and constantly asked questions. Soon I was writing a series of fifty-two half-hour programmes, operating the equipment for others, helping with follow-up, and anything else I was asked to do.

I still had links with Crusaders and helped lead the local class for my first few years at Radio Worldwide. I also spoke at other classes, young people's weekends, and summer houseparties.

After four years I ran out of steam. The doctor said I was suffering from nervous exhaustion, but friends feared I had had a breakdown. I felt as though I was cut off from the real me, caged in a corner, unable to do anything. The following three months at home were dark, but in them I learned vital lessons, particularly about why I had reached such a low ebb.

In my diary I later listed various reasons:

★ To escape, especially from loneliness.

★ As a compensation. Because I'm not married, I feel myself to be a failure in that area, therefore I *must* succeed in my job.

★ To prove myself to God. He has called me to this work, so I subconsciously feel the need to prove to Him that I can do it.

★ So that others need me. If I'm the most efficient, most available, or quickest person at any particular job, I will be 'needed' to do that, and I need to be needed by someone.

★ Because I cannot say 'No'. The Lord doesn't want me to take on every job that's offered to me, or meet every need I see. Doing things He doesn't want me to only drains my reserves of strength.

★ I cannot trust others. I hang on to jobs that others should be doing, or check up on things they are doing that are none of my business. I don't trust them, or the Lord in them, and a breakdown in fellowship results.

★ As an unconscious effort to compete with those with whom I work.

★ It boosts my pride to be seen to be working hard. It also sometimes brings sympathy and attention.

★ For fear of criticism. It's hard to say 'No' or appear to let someone down.

★ I was too busy to spend time asking the Lord why I was too busy!

Help! What on earth was a person like this doing as a missionary? Yet God did not show me these things to condemn me, but because He

wanted to set me free from them. God's desire is
to make us more like Christ, but so often He has
to show us what we are really like before we will
let Him radically change our lives.

The way up

Over the following years I slowly applied some
of these lessons. But there was one area I could
not come to terms with — being single. I live with
families, so I know all about the disadvantages of
being married. I hear the baby crying at some
awful hour of the night, and turn over, glad I do
not have to drag myself out into the cold. I see the
mothers wanting to do so much more in the team,
but unable to because of children. On the other
hand, I would go out to a recording session with
others, and sometimes come home late, tired and
hungry. I would watch the married ones go into a
warm, lighted flat, while I climbed the stairs to a
cold, dark room. I hated it, it seemed so unfair.
Somehow God had to meet me in this area too.

He did so the year some of us thought Radio
Worldwide might close because four of our senior
members moved on to other ministries. At that
time I tore some ligaments in my back. For six
weeks I could not even sit down, and it was longer
before I could drive again. I pleaded with the
Lord to heal me as He had done on other occasions.
Instead He began to teach me deeper lessons.

One day the pain, and the frustration about the
future, almost drove me to the end of my tether. I
was complaining bitterly to someone who suddenly said, "The trouble with you is you're afraid
of the future." I knew God had spoken to me. In
the next few days He revealed that the root of the
fear went right back to the time of my birth.

When I was born both my mother and I were critically ill, so for weeks I was only picked up to be fed or changed. Right there my insecurity and rejection had begun.

When God opened up the deep wounds it was unbelievably painful. But He quickly poured in His love and peace. For the first time I was able to come to terms with being single. Gone was the heavy weight that for years had been stopping me from running freely in the race set before me. What a difference it made! Not only did I feel a new person, others quickly recognised it too. Within weeks God showed the Radio Worldwide team that I was to be the next leader!

Since then I have begun to learn many new lessons: the authority we have as sons of God; coping with relationships; being a woman in leadership.

Over the years there have been the touches of God's love too: He provided a friend who sends me beautiful clothes, such as I would never buy for myself. So I do not need to look like the stereotyped missionaries I met as a teenager! Above all, I know that as I remain obedient to God and willing to accept His discipline in my life, He will continue to lead me onward.

Points to Ponder:
1. Do you do just enough to be looked on as a 'good Christian', or have you really made Jesus the Lord of your whole life?
2. Secure or insecure? Is there some area of your past that still needs to be opened to God's loving, healing touch?

Relevant scriptures:
1. Matthew 7:21-29.
2. Luke 19:1-10, Psalm 139.

12

TO BRAZIL — AND THE WORLD — WITH LOVE

Robert Harvey

Lesson one: The need for witness at home

Ever since I became a Christian I've enjoyed encouraging people. But it took me twenty years to realise that God had given me this gift of encouragement for the building up of His church. But let me go back to the beginning.

The real beginning came two years after I first accepted Christ on the evening of 31 August, 1955. For those two years I had kept silent at home where, as the only son, I was afraid of spoiling the family unity by speaking about the Lord. I loved Him though, and devoured His Word, both at home (under the bed covers with a torch), and at High School during the midday lunch break which I spent in the park.

There He led me to the Song of Solomon 3:4: "I held Him and would not let him go till I had brought him to my mother's house . . ." "Bob, do you love me?" He asked. Of course I loved Him!

"Then take me home to your mother and father." Oh, how I battled with Him! But finally, captured by the love of Jesus, I returned home to share my new Lord with my loved ones. Yes, He captured me to do His will, anywhere, any time, whatever it was, at any price.

Lesson two: The right priorities

"Any price"? Beverley and I had been going together for two years before we felt we had to make some decision about the future. Both school teachers, with a clear missionary call burning in our hearts, we were determined not to get engaged until God showed each of us, separately, where He wanted us to work. God had used Pat Symes, a pioneer WEC missionary to Colombia, to call Bev. He used Douglas Anderson, a missionary from the Lebanese Evangelical Mission, to call me. Did God want her in Colombia and me in the Middle East?

A year before this, in 1962, Leslie Brierley, the International Research Secretary of the WEC, had made a survey trip to Brazil. His findings, published in a detailed report, indicated that Brazil was on the eve of a worldwide missionary thrust. By some strange coincidence this document fell into our hands and God used it to lead us both — quite separately. How thrilled we were when we each shared our guidance, and discovered that the Lord wanted us in Brazil together!

Lesson three: The reward of patience

Cabin 216 of the Italian liner *Castle Felice*, on its final voyage to Europe, wasn't exactly a palace, but it was to be our home for forty-seven days. In contact with people of many nations, God burned into our hearts a determination to learn Portuguese as well as we could, in order to communicate Christ. We learned patience too, for the 'Six Day War' broke out and we had to sail round Africa rather than go through the Suez Canal to Britain! From there the *Arlanza*, a Royal Mail Line ship, was to take us to our promised land.

We enjoyed two weeks at the former WEC headquarters in south-east London. We also enjoyed two weeks of glorious summer weather wearing our Aussie shorts and thongs (horrors for the English). It was all we needed to prepare us for the next lap, and our fourth equatorial crossing in two months.

Lesson four: The trials of adjustment

There were no medals for drinking the strong, black, sweet coffee on the *Arlanza*, but nevertheless it helped us to identify immediately with the Brazilians, because the *cafezinho* is a very important part of their culture. That wasn't the only thing we had to learn in Brazil though! There was the language with its strange nasal sounds, and gestures, different food and spices, different values for space and sound, and above all, the strange religious superstitions which were a mixture of African, Indian and Portuguese (Roman Catholic) thinking. Often at a crossroads we would see a burning candle, a plate of food, a bottle of whisky and a slain chicken — evidence of witchcraft put there to do harm to someone.

But besides all this, we had to learn how to cope with a new baby boy, a brother for Kathy, aged two. Then hepatitis hit me, with pain under the tenth rib, right side. I was more yellow than a Chinaman, but still we kept on with language study. Bev had had one day in hospital to give birth to Andy and next day was home and into the language again. What a party! It was the rainy season too, and the quaint tiled roof of our little lean-to house just filtered the rain for us. We had all kinds of things hanging from the ceiling to stop the drips falling on to the beds, the babies, and us!

We can see the funny side of it all now, but I must confess it wasn't easy at the time.

Months passed. We wanted to begin challenging people about missions. But this wasn't yet part of the missionary team's vision, so we just had to bide our time. Getting nearer the people, to understand them and identify with them was a must, so we were led into evangelism and church planting, first among a poor, simple, country people and then in an educated, religious, cultured town. What extremes! It was God's wonderful way of preparing us for contacts with the poor and the cultured from north, south, east and west.

I'll never forget the week we moved out of our comfortable mission house in Manga, to live and work with the desperately poor people at Prai, a little village forty-five minutes up-river.

Our bedroom had a number of inmates: mosquitoes at night, bedbugs, fleas, chickens looking for their breakfast at the corn pile in the corner, barber-bugs (in the crevices in the mud walls), which transmit a fatal disease called *Chaga*, and us! The days were very busy, starting with early breakfast with wild honey, freshly-boiled milk and tapioca porridge (no sugar, of course), or manioc flour cakes. There were no bathrooms or toilets so we went into the river for a bath and behind the corn stalks for the other.

Lesson five: The value of identification

How the nationals laughed at me as I joined them in their farm work! I couldn't distinguish wild rice from the genuine article. It reminded me of the wheat and the tares! We sweated, laughed, grew callouses on our hands and became weary, alongside the locals. This identification opened their hearts to us. In the evenings they gathered from all round to listen to consecutive teaching, and on the last night there came a breakthrough. One of the leading young men in the community, married, intelligent, outspoken and dynamic, spoke out, "I want to accept Christ as my Saviour and Lord." Hallelujah! Today he is the pastor of the church with a tremendous teaching ministry. Recently he invited us back for some meetings. Twenty years later folk still talk about those precious times of fellowship.

Lesson six: The fire of opposition

From Manga to Mariana! Deep-rooted catholicism with dozens of churches, two seminaries, a convent, a Bishop's residence, a developed educational system, lawyers, doctors, and refined Portuguese culture were a bigger shock to our system than the move from Australia to Brazil. Of course our presence was a shock to them. We would never have thought that two humble Australians could cause such a rumpus!

"After 274 years of existence, the time has come for our historic archiepiscopal city, Mariana, to receive within her walls a Protestant penetration force. In our beloved city we now have the novelty of a Protestant meeting led by a young gentleman from an evangelical cult. ... Let us see if this young propagandist obtains followers for his Christianity, without sacraments and without the loving and protective presence of the Virgin Mary...." (So said an article from a Roman Catholic newspaper distributed Brazil-wide.) None of these things moved us, and the work went on! Recently the pastor in Mariana invited us back to share at the now independent church there.

Lesson seven: The fulfilment of a vision

Surprise! Who should arrive in Brazil but Leslie Brierley, anxious to see his vision of 1962, of an army of Brazilian missionaries moving out into the world, become reality. He did a grand job, and even today we are still reaping the fruits of his dedicated ministry. But the International Office wanted him back, his visa was expiring and he was praying, "Lord, raise up someone younger to take up this challenge." Little did he know that that someone was right there with him in the WEC team. He was jubilant when we told him, and immediate plans were made for us to begin our first 'Missionary Orientation Course' in January 1974, after furlough in Britain and Australia. Leslie never returned but the course went ahead.

Doors began to open in Bible Schools, seminaries, conferences and churches, and we were able to share the challenge of "The whole wide world for Jesus". We tried to encourage the formation of Brazilian sending agencies too, and the Lord raised up leaders who have taken tremendous initiative both in promoting missions among the churches and sending out workers.

At last our Brazil field became a *sending base*, with Brazilian WEC Missionaries integrating with our international teams in Italy, Spain, Portugal, Sri Lanka, Zaire, Japan, Senegal and Guinea-Bissau. And there's more to come in the future!

Twenty years ago, the night before we were interviewed by the WEC candidate committee in Sydney, Australia, God said to us, "As I was with Moses, so I will be with you. Do not be afraid!" How wonderful that He continues to whisper that in our ears and, as Brazilians join us, He is saying it to them too. Hallelujah!

Points to Ponder:
1. How ready are you, mentally and spiritually, to suffer for the sake of the gospel?
2. Are you prepared to wait for God's time for the fulfilment of what He has said to you?

Relevant scriptures:
1. 1 Peter 4:1, 2 Corinthians 4:8-12.
2. Habakkuk 2:1-4.

13

OUT OF MY PUDDLE INTO HIS SEA

Mady Vaillant

Will you trust Me fully?

The book gripped me, I could not put it down. Through Mary Slessor's life story the Lord was speaking to me. Soon my little attic room became the place of my surrender to Him as both Saviour and Lord. I was only fifteen but I knew deep down that He was calling me to serve Him in Africa. That was an unheard of thing in our little French Evangelical Church. Some time later, when I talked about Bible School training, the elders backed my mother in trying to dissuade me.

It was the beginning of a long journey with my Lord. As we walked together I learned to recognise His voice. One of His first questions to me was, "Will you fully trust Me as we journey together?"

There was plenty of opportunity to do just that. My parents were separated. Whilst my mother, younger brother and I were living together, my father lived in another part of the town on his own. When we accidentally met I could not bring myself to talk to him. I felt he had wronged my mother so much. But as I prayed about Bible School, one thing became clear: the Lord wanted to work in my parents' lives before He would give me the green light for Bible School. I knew father wasn't good at keeping house, and one day the

Lord said, "Why not greet him next time you see him and ask him if you can go and clean the house?" I gulped. Impossible! "Will you just trust Me to open the way?" He did! From then on, once a week, I found myself before a mountain of dishes to wash. Slowly the Lord worked, and one day I witnessed the reconciliation of my parents. When I saw them kneeling together in the sitting room, asking the Lord to give them a new start, I knew the way to Bible School was open.

After three years in Bible School, the call to Africa became very faint. Why? Because so few French young men seemed to be interested in the mission field! Opportunities to serve the Lord in France were numerous. Why go so far?

I started to work for an evangelistic newspaper in Paris, but God's voice kept asking, "Won't you trust Me to be your all, to be to you even more than a husband would be?" It took three years, but in the end I said, "Yes, Lord".

I was accepted by WEC for Upper Volta (now Burkina Faso). When I came home my mother said, "This life of faith, making your needs known to God only, is all right in England where Christians know about it, but it will never work in France. The few French missionaries there are have a salary. Everybody will believe you have one too." That was logical thinking. But God said, "Will you trust Me for finance too?" That was twenty-five years ago. He has never let me down. He has always provided in time, even if my faith has sometimes been stretched to the limit.

Will you let Me refine you?

God had already started His refining process at home. On the mission field He began to refine even more. There were personality clashes with no way of escaping, because we were trapped on the same station. The purifying fire burned deeply. I never knew the dross was so abundant!

The tensions had been growing steadily between another missionary and myself. As usual I could see where he was wrong, and I guess he saw where I was wrong too. As the days went by I knew I was growing spiritually cold. Then it was my turn to preach in an outchurch far away in the bush. The whole day the Lord spoke to me about repentance. On the way back the motorbike broke down. I could not mend it, and who should be dispatched to my help but that very brother. I could hold back no longer; there and then I repented of my critical attitude. As so often is the case, when my defences went down, so did his. The Lord met us, melted us and enabled us to work together for many years. Together we opened a Bible School in Bouroum-Bouroum.

This refining process still goes on. Having lived with some ten different co-workers, I thought I was well 'run in'. The Lord knew better. This term He has put me with an easy-going, forgetful type of co-worker. Suddenly I have come to realise I have had an idol in my heart. Its creed goes something like this, "I believe in the god called efficiency!" This idol, like any other, has had to be brought to the light, renounced and destroyed. Not that efficiency is wrong, but love to God and to my neighbour must have priority over it.

For some years I have heard another of His direct questions:

Will you enter with Me into spiritual warfare?

I was not too sure. Doesn't one get hurt in warfare? He was very gentle but firm. First, as I responded, He began to work in me to bring about spiritual release. For instance, I was too self-conscious when it came to praising Him publicly. When I was on furlough, one Sunday He dealt with that self-consciousness. In the morning meeting people had been praising the Lord freely, even raising their hands to Him in worship and adoration. That was not for me! But when the Holy Spirit is quenched a special sadness comes upon us. "Lord, I could never do that!" I said. "Will you trust Me?" the Lord replied. In the evening meeting the invitation was given to simply open one's hands on one's lap, as a sign that we wanted to receive all that the Lord had for us. Before I knew it my hands shot up. There was such a release of love and praise to the Lord!

Later on, He dealt with fears that had held me for a long time. I knew without the shadow of a doubt that He had delivered me when, coming back sick from the South of France, I had to drive in the night all around Paris in the pelting rain, not knowing the way too well. I was alone in the car. No, He was there too! Suddenly I realised I was not the least afraid, and I could sing with joy at my release from fear.

Back on the field, He is now giving me opportunity to enter into spiritual warfare and to see others released from the bondage of the enemy. Our team of six (four Africans and two missionaries) are all learners in this, but the Lord is teaching us step by step. We are learning how to listen to His Holy Spirit, to pray with authority, to add fasting to prayer, and so on. When Kirdjir (a man possessed by many evil spirits) was brought to us, he had to be tied up because he was often violent.

As we ministered to him, chain after chain of spiritual bondage was identified and broken in the name of Jesus. He is not the only one, but those who are released have to learn to walk in their new freedom, and not all of them have managed it.

Will you follow Me on uncharted paths?

Three years ago I was approached about field leadership. My first reaction was, "I can't do it, not as a single woman." That was a totally uncharted path for me. However I heard His voice again, "Will you trust Me?" As a love token He gave me Deuteronomy 31:8. In the French Bible it says, "The Lord *Himself* shall go before you, He *Himself* shall be with you . . ." With this clear promise of His own presence with me I could go forward. As I saw it, the challenge was for me to come out of my 'puddle' and dive into the limitless sea of His resources, to let Him lead through me.

As I am opening up to this ocean of resources, several things are coming into focus. I am to have faith in the total work of the Cross. Not only have all my sins been freely forgiven, but I am also crucified with Him to my sinful nature. He now lives in me, the container. I am also to have faith in His supernatural way of working, even if it leads me into unknown territories. I am to submit to Him in everything, and to submit to what He shows me through His Body, the Church.

The other day I went alone into the town of Gaoua with the mission truck. Coming to a muddy stretch I took the detour that supposedly was better than the actual road and got stuck in the mud. I tried all the tricks I knew: gathering small rocks to pave the way, cutting branches to push under the wheels and so on, but the more I tried to get out on my own the more firmly the truck got stuck.

As my feet and legs sunk into the muck, all that I had learned about bilharziasis, Guinea worm and other parasites, came back to mind. I prayed for someone to come along, but at first only a middle-aged woman came. Later on a man appeared. We both tried to get the truck out, but to no avail. The man went away to call others. It took six strong men to get the truck back on firm ground! As I sped away rejoicing, I saw this as a parable. The more I try to get out of my weak spots, the more deeply I sink. I need the help of Christ and that of my brothers and sisters in the Body.

"Lord, I believe you have taught me this lesson before, but in my present circumstances I was inclined to forget it. Forgive me; and keep me from being so busy with your work that I do not have enough time to spend at Your feet, listening to Your voice."

Points to Ponder:
1. Are you able to trust God in all the circumstances of life, including any difficulty you may be facing right now?
2. Have you ever tried praising the Lord (a) when things go wrong, and (b) when something happens that upsets you personally? What result did you experience in yourself?

Relevant scriptures:
1. Psalm 34:1-4, Jonah 2:4-10.
2. Psalm 42.

SECTION 4

GAINING BY GIVING

14

IT CAN'T HAPPEN IN SOUTH SUMATRA!

Werner Jahnke

A strange birthday present

My birthday! On the table is a Bible. The guests at the small party looked at the presents and also at the Bible, but no one talked about it, because not one of them reads this strange old-fashioned book.

After everyone had gone I picked up the Bible and started to read. As with other books, I started with the first page. As time went by I spent two or three hours every day reading it. I saw a remarkable story unfolding — the story of God's dealings with His people. There were many things I didn't understand, but I went on. Very soon I came to a crisis. There had been no God in my life before reading this book, but now He stood before me. I saw that mankind is divided into two large groups. One is going to eternal punishment, the other to eternal life. How will God divide the people? It was a difficult question, and I had no immediate answer. Where would God (if there is a God) put me? The answer was simple but shocking: I was on the road to judgment.

After four months of pondering the Scriptures, I made a clear decision. Starting that day, I would live according to the will of God as revealed in His

Word. Maybe I didn't understand too much about the saving power of Christ, but He heard my cry for salvation and I know I was accepted by Him. At that very moment I thought about the many who didn't know anything about the law of God. They are all on the road to eternal punishment too. I didn't know anything about missions, but I felt something should be done to reach these many lost people in the world.

Into deeper waters

Later the Lord led me to the Adelshofen Bible school in Southern Germany. There I learned many lessons, such as the need for:

Brokenness in my life in order to be fruitful.

Keeping on in prayer, with faith, to overcome all obstacles. (We spent many hours in prayer for the needs of the school and for the many who have not yet been reached with the gospel.)

Regarding others much higher than myself.

A knowledge of spiritual warfare as we face, not merely difficult human beings, but the powers of darkness which control them. They can only be destroyed if we are ready to fight on a spiritual plain.

To have victory in all kinds of temptations.

To know His Word thoroughly and to become a doer of His will.

The ability to live together with others, especially if, in my opinion, they hold strange views.

My whole life to be given to evangelisation, so that every aspect of my life will contribute to the saving of souls for the Lord.

One other important lesson came to me from the reading of a book about George Müller. His life of faith really challenged me, and I started to trust the Lord for my personal needs. But very soon I received a much greater challenge. I became the treasurer of the small and little-known Bible school. Now I had to learn to trust the Lord for the daily needs of the school, for funds for a building programme and for the outreach of the school. I had many precious experiences during that time. We saw the Lord stepping in when we didn't have any solution. He was always greater than the problem! This period laid a firm foundation in my life.

Not just Germany

From the beginning of my Christian life I had a vision for spreading the gospel, but I had no knowledge of mission work.

Missionary magazines, conferences and many books helped me to get a clear picture about mission. I learned about the tremendous needs in this world, and the ways and means of reaching people who are without Christ. I saw very clearly that the man who is sent by God plays a key role in the whole matter.

Soon I was ready to dedicate my whole life for missionary enterprise, but I was not yet ready to go. I had two excuses. First, I spoke very poor English. Even though I had tried to learn it I had not made much headway. I thought that if I went to the mission field I would have to learn not only English but at least one other language, maybe one even more difficult than English! The second reason was that I was hardly able to stand a hot summer in Germany. If I couldn't stand the heat of Germany, I would never cope in the tropics, so it was impossible for me to become a missionary! I consoled myself with the need for people at home to back up the missionaries, and this is what I was going to do. But I had no peace in my heart.

One day the pressure of the Spirit was so strong that I knelt down in my room and said to the Lord, "If You send me to the Tuaregs in the Sahara (Tuaregs have a very difficult language and the Sahara is a really hot place!) I am ready to go. If I die in a year and I never present the gospel to anyone, that is Your responsibility, but I'll go." I stood up with a wonderful peace in my heart.

God's green light

For the past sixteen years I have lived in Indonesia. How kind of the Lord to send me to a country with an easy language! I was able to learn Indonesian and can speak it fluently. My wife and I are living in a tropical climate, but the Lord has kept me alive, even though I do have many difficulties with the heat.

I was invited to attend a Christian wedding in a remote area of Southern Sumatra. The car driver who took me there was a doctor responsible for the clinics in a wide area. Whenever we went through a village, I asked him, "How many have come to know the Lord in this village? How is the church growing here?" He always answered, "As far as I know there is no Christian witness in this village!" Then I asked him about other places that I had seen on the map. His answer was, "As far as I know there is no Christian witness in those places either." I wondered who would ever take the gospel to these people.

When we finally arrived at the wedding village, I looked for a quiet place to prepare, as it had already been decided that I should bring the message in the wedding ceremony. But it was very difficult to concentrate. I heard again and again the voice in my ear, "As far as I know there is no Christian witness." In that quiet corner God showed me that Southern Sumatra was the place for me, because there were wide areas untouched by the gospel. I read Isaiah 42:1-10 and I saw that these verses fitted the situation in that large area, with its tremendous needs and shortage of workers.

My wife, Else, ran a clinic in a remote area. Hundreds of Muslims came for treatment. I had to learn to share the gospel simply with people who had never before heard it. This confrontation with a new culture challenged my understanding of Jesus Christ. I discovered that He is unique — the answer to mankind's many questions, including those of the Islamic village folk in South Sumatra.

One bad banana

A village elder once explained to me that in the last days there will be a pair of scales. On one side God will place all the good deeds, and on the other all the wrong doings. The elder was quite sure that he had more good deeds than bad ones.

I asked him, "What about your bananas? You put a hundred in a basket, and one is rotten. But there is no problem because ninety-nine are stronger than one."

"Oh, no, if you do not remove the rotten one, all will become rotten."

"But ninety-nine are more than one, aren't they?"

"You can be sure, if the rotten one is not removed, all will be rotten."

"That's strange! These bananas don't seem to follow the law of the scales. And what about this boat here? It is ten metres long. Imagine that in the middle is a hole of ten centimetres. Surely the ten centimetres are stronger than ten metres! Or what about a thief, when he goes on trial? He says to the judge, 'Weigh carefully! For one thousand days I was a good man. Only on the one night when I was caught, did I do something wrong.' There is no such weighing in the courtroom. The thief will be judged according to his crimes.

"Take another example. Think about a plate with wonderful food on it. Ninety-nine per cent of it is halal (religiously clean)."

"Then it is not halal, it is haram (religiously unclean)."

"But I would like to ask you, how can this dish become halal, so that we can eat it?"

"There is no way; throw it away!"

"But you have just explained to me that you hope that your good deeds will outweigh your sins. That means you have sinned."

"Yes, there is no man without sin."

"But sin is haram. How can you stand before God with your sins? In this world there is no trading of good deeds for sin, no halal for haram. How can you hope that there will be this kind of trading on the judgment day?"

Silence! The man was shocked. After a time he asked, "But how can we be saved?"

Then came the wonderful moment when I explained to him God's way of salvation. Later we were able to share the message with ten thousand people. Now we can speak about the gospel, eternal life, grace and forgiveness. Some have been converted and are faithful members of the church. Others have believed in Christ, but have not joined any church.

Multiplying the ministry

In my Bible studies I have spoken many times about trials in our lives. One day I had a heart attack by the road side, far from the nearest hospital. I had wonderful peace during that time and was able to pray to the Lord. I had three attacks and after that had to stay at home, unable to do anything. Later I had a terrible pain in my left leg. But all this worked together for good; I could better understand the words of Job, "The LORD gave and the LORD has taken away; may the name of the Lord be praised." Then we received a cable that Else's father had suddenly died. But in the midst of all this we experienced the Lord as our Comforter.

A young man received Christ in our home at the very time that Else's father was being buried back in Germany! Through all these trials, we were brought nearer to the Lord and from this background we are much more able to minister to people with many needs.

The Lord leads on. Now we help at a theological seminary training young people. Some students are now entering the villages, making contact with the villagers, and being invited back. So we are multipliers, teaching evangelism in such a way that many more will become personal evangelists.

Points to Ponder:
1. Does your vision extend beyond your own country to a whole world waiting for the gospel?
2. Have you ever considered the difficulties of presenting the gospel to someone of a different culture? Do you know such a person with whom you could share?

Relevant scriptures:
1. Matthew 28:19-20, 1 Timothy 2:1.
2. 1 Corinthians 9:16-22.

15

YOU DON'T BELONG TO YOURSELF

Marie Dinnen

Early memories

"I know the waitresses pool their tips and share them out each week, but I won't be here when they do the share-out, so I'll just pocket mine." As a teenager I was serving in the hotel-restaurant of family friends, who had taken me under their wing for music tuition. However, my conscience troubled me about this pilfering at the time, and for long afterwards. Eventually I had to write confessing my sin and making restitution.

My very earliest memories are of an almost idyllic life centred round a country manse in the north islands of Scotland. A steady routine of school, church and family activity, slanted to our rural setting, gave a sense of security. In my early teens the foundations of God's Word laid in my life began to bear fruit. It became clear to me that I couldn't enter heaven on my parents' passport. My capitulation to Christ came through an unshakable conviction that God alone had the right to direct and control my life. I thank God for my parents who exposed me to His Word and taught me obedience; then for the two people whom God used specifically to convince me of His Lordship, our family doctor and a Faith Mission pilgrim.

100% or nothing

An inbuilt tendency never to do things by halves enabled me to pitch into Christian living with gusto and determination, intent on serving God with all my heart. But the more I desired to be like Him and be worthy of Him, the more aware I became of sin, selfishness and separation from God. My idealistic, perfectionist nature did not want to accept what I really was, but God's Holy Spirit sharpened this awareness and faithfully dealt with issues as they surfaced. Over a period of time I came to a fuller realisation of what Paul meant when he said, "I have been crucified with Christ and I no longer live, but Christ lives in me" (Galatians 2:20). The day came when I could write in my Bible over Romans 6, "I am finished", and really mean it. But it took some drastic dealings and honest facing up to issues of sins of body, mind and spirit before release came. It was at this time that I wrote making confession of the restaurant pilfering.

I had plenty of ambition and was aiming high in life before God got hold of me. As a Christian, scripture impressed on me that the cross must be laid on every aspect of life. Jesus didn't please Himself, but did only what His Father wanted. Eventually I was able to pray, "Lord, what do *You* want me to do?" My plan was to become a medical missionary in India. God's plan cut right across mine and led into nursing, Bible training and service in the homelands.

Conscious of inbuilt gifts for organisation and administration, I could have capitulated to the pressures of nursing superiors to proceed to the Royal College of Nursing and an administrative post. But at that time a WEC worker challenged me. "There is no gift, natural or spiritual, that we lay at the feet of Jesus, but that He raises to use in power in the way He wants." From the time of that surrender until now, I can see how God harnessed this potential and used it, first in administration in our WEC Missionary College, and more recently in the implementation of lay Bible study ministry across the world. Instead of Marie Dinnen doing her own individual thing, hundreds of young lives have been channelled into Christian service at home and abroad, and thousands of lay persons encouraged to disciple others in outreach Bible study groups.

A bondslave owns nothing! Being willing for discipleship is one thing. Being prepared for it another. Once I had realised I had no rights, it became easier to handle individual issues as they came up, but there had to be realistic facing up to each one. He made me willing to face life without a partner then gave the one of His choice. He made me willing to forego a family in the interests of being totally free to serve, and then after five years of marriage gave us two children.

Through these lessons I came to see that even what He has given me is not mine. My husband belongs to Him first; that sets ministry priorities right. My children are a trust from Him; that puts me under an obligation to lay spiritual principles in their lives and to release them to His purposes. The safeguard in this for me is that it enables me to fully roll the responsibility of my children's lives on to Him and obviates me playing God. Ultimately they are responsible to Him, not me, for their choices.

Saved deep down and every day

As I grew spiritually I also realised that the seed-thought of sin in my heart was just as bad as the action. When our first child was born she suffered cerebral irritation. This resulted in our days becoming tension-filled and 'sleeping' hours a nightmare. The situation was further compounded when a second child arrived two years later. One woke the other and I despaired of ever having a reasonable night's sleep. My nerves were jangled. On one occasion when my husband was away for several weeks lecturing, I became so desperate that I sat up in bed crying, "Oh God, do something before I harm these children!" At that moment my husband walked into the room! He had hitched a four-hundred-mile ride to be with us for his free weekend! Later, God delivered our daughter of this affliction, but I had learned my lesson. There are no degrees of sin with God.

The wear and tear of close interchange with fellow workers highlights yet deeper needs. The way to vital, productive fellowship is the way of openness and brokenness. When these don't prevail, calamity can result. After twelve years on our mission staff I found myself the victim of gross misunderstanding and false accusation. I wanted to stand up and cry out, "I am innocent," but God whispered to me that Jesus was silent when He was falsely accused. Out of that devastating experience, when everything of spiritual worth seemed reduced to ashes, God brought me to the peace of knowing that I was dead and my life was hid with Christ in God. Out of this came a glorious resurrection and some of the most joyous and fruitful years of ministry.

No let up

It is easy to condense and make these statements, but I have only come to reality in each area through breakings, heart searchings, prayer, relinquishment, and believing His promises. The devil would trick us and pursue us even into old age, seeking to get us to deviate from the way of the cross. Recently, facing a change of commission and a transfer across the world, he sought to rattle me on the issue of retirement. Had I not served God wholeheartedly down the years? Shouldn't I be taking things a little easier now?

Someone in Australia had left a home to WEC earmarked for our use in retirement years. Now, I'm a home lover at heart, and having lived communally all my life, I would dearly love a quiet corner of my own. Opting for independent action at this point would have been easy. But the red light was flashing. "You don't belong to yourself. What does God want?" Thank God for a proven path! The house went. The Lord won. God provided a place for us on the other side of the world and we are happy in the task He has given us to do.

The issue of family was not so easy to settle. Our obedience to God had landed our girls on a new continent away from close family links. They both had little children and our older daughter was not at all well. Wouldn't I be a heel to walk out on that responsibility? Years before I had come to terms with Christ's demand that we put Him before parents and children. It was one thing to leave parents for His sake. But children? And grandchildren? "Lord Jesus, whatever You want is best. If You take me overseas, I can trust the family to You, but please show me beyond a shadow of doubt where my present priority lies." He did.

Gaining by giving

The Bible is very specific about spiritual investment. Years ago, facing a ministry in a 'faith' mission didn't seem to pose a problem for me. Maybe I was initially carried along by natural enthusiasm. But enthusiasm doesn't produce bread and butter. The testimony of WEC missionaries, totally abandoned to God and proving Him the all sufficient One, coupled with scripture, led to a simple expectancy that, if I obeyed, He would not fail me. Again, I learned through practical experience.

My army officer husband had accrued quite a fat bank book while on service overseas in World War II. The natural thing was to open a joint account with his penniless nurse fianceé. Instead, we released the cash to His control and He channelled it to others. I did have a tussle over wedding present money. Wasn't it mine? How nicely we could furnish our barren quarters in the Missionary Training College in Scotland! That went too, to provide furnishings for a newly-acquired college extension. One hour later someone rang and said, "Please go and order furnishings for your apartment. Get everything you need. I will pay the bill." God is no man's debtor! For almost forty years God has continually met our needs, both large and small, for personal and ministry purposes.

If financial investment for Christ pays off, how productive is investment in lives? Being a Martha by nature, I love action. I delighted to work alongside missionary trainees in their practical sessions. Eventually God stopped me in my tracks and challenged me to train others to teach. Bit by bit He enabled me to relinquish areas of responsibility until I had worked myself out of a job. But what was to take its place?

Quite spontaneously, through counselling a neighbour in need, an evangelistic Bible study was commenced in our lounge. The ministry grew rapidly, and once again I found myself having to relinquish tasks I loved. Areas of responsibility were handed to others as the Lord freed me for expansion, city wide, then state wide, continent wide and finally world wide. God's addition is by multiplication! He was again rechannelling that old gift of organisation and administration for His purposes and glory. Now the *Geared for Growth* ministry incorporates a team of writers, national co-ordinators, leaders and thousands of group members around the world. Groups operate in English, Dutch, Spanish, French, Finnish, German, Korean, Malaysian, Tamil, Javanese, Portuguese, Chinese, Eket and other Nigerian languages. The work is presently being launched in Zambia, Zimbabwe, Austria and, we trust, Greece.

The secret? Spiritual investment in obedience to God's Word. The foundation principle of the *Word Worldwide* is contained in Proverbs 11:24,25, which groups use as their motto. It might be paraphrased like this:

"It is possible to give away and become richer.
It is also possible to hold on too tightly and
lose everything.
Yes, the liberal man shall be rich.
By watering others, he waters himself."

Points to Ponder:
1. Have you surrendered your natural gifts and abilities to Jesus, or are you still trying to organise your Christian service around them?

2. Do you feel justified in taking things a bit easier now because (a) you are older, and (b) you made sacrifices for Jesus in earlier years?

3. What place should spiritual gifts have in determining your pattern and place of service?

Relevant scriptures:
1 & 3. Romans 12:3-11.
2. 2 Timothy 4:6-8.

16

PROVING GOD FINANCIALLY

Philip & Nancy Wood

It's all Yours, Lord!

Looking back over fourteen years in Africa we are amazed to see how God has led us on in the matter of finance. We can now say, "It's all Yours, Lord! We don't have any financial problems. We don't have any money, because it's all Yours."

Before leaving Canada to study tropical medicine, only one person specifically promised to stand behind us financially. Obviously there were other very faithful friends who supported us because we have never lacked, but the fellow who promised has never given us anything!

Like all new missionary candidates we were eager to reach the mission field just as soon as possible, but two months before our proposed departure date we had received only one gift towards our fares. At that time a senior worker gave a challenge to all in WEC Headquarters. "Tithe your gifts and see the blessing of the Lord!" The mission's general fund was low that month. We discussed this together and realised we had not tithed the money that we had received. So we took a cheque along to the finance office. It wasn't easy or logical to give away some of what we had, when we needed so much more in just two months. That afternoon Philip was very surprised to be called to Reception to see the treasurer from his church. He explained that a large gift had been put in the offering plate the previous Sunday earmarked for us, and he wanted to deliver it to us in person!

A thousand miles from help?

We reached the capital of Zaire but were still more than a thousand miles from the nearest WEC missionary. We were delayed there about six weeks getting our official papers to practise medicine. We had had one gift from Nancy's home church in Canada, but had not heard whether they would support our missionary work regularly, so we were surprised to receive their telegram to say that a significant sum of money had been transferred to a large bank in Kinshasa for our needs. Already familiar with Zaire's inefficiency and bureaucracy, we were amazed when we located the bank and found that their documents really *did* show that sum of money in our name! With a delay of not more than an hour we were able to withdraw it.

We have always been very happy with the WEC policy that we should look to the Lord for our needs, and not to the mission or even to our home church. He has always seen that all our needs were met, and has enabled us to take on various projects, including sending a national colleague to study in London for a year. At the same time God led us on to trust Him for the finance for our new house in Nyankunde. We had been living in a mud and thatch house built by Dr Helen Roseveare, which became inadequate for a family with children and for the many guests who began to travel from North America and Europe via Nairobi and Nyankunde. We had to trust the Lord for the finance for a permanent brick house. When we first mentioned the project, our builder thought it would cost $8,000. In six months the Lord had provided just that amount. By the time the foundation was laid, the estimate had gone up to $11,000. But when the first bills started to come in we could see that the final cost would be much higher. Philip began to worry about where all that money would come from, not to mention the funds for going on furlough six months later, but the Lord provided that money well in advance.

Looking to God alone

Just to reinforce the lesson the Lord was teaching us, the pastors of our respective churches at home resigned. Both were very gifted preachers: Philip's church in Guildford had grown phenomenally, as had Nancy's in Toronto. It seemed that the allowances these churches were giving us would be bound to drop. However, the Lord was reminding us to look to Him and not even to our faithful home churches. We returned from furlough and moved into our new house. When all the bills were paid our house had cost us $32,000 and we always had had money in hand. The final payment was made the month we moved in. We received many special gifts, including $2,000 from ranchers in Alberta whom we have never met and have not been able to trace.

While on furlough in Canada, Nancy was hospitalised three times when our second son threatened to come early, and in all had to spend sixty-six days in hospital, thirty-one of them in intensive care. Although we had not been in Canada for eight years, it was possible to reactivate Nancy's old insurance which covered all but

$20 of the bills which arose out of her hospitalisation and Timothy's premature birth. The bills exceeded $20,000! We had non-refundable return tickets to England and Africa which we were unable to use because of the medical problems, but we had travel insurance. The insurance did not cover pregnancies, but we were able to show that we bought the insurance before Nancy was pregnant and the insurance company paid for new tickets, including one for Timothy who hadn't possessed one in the first place! And in the medical problems the Lord again proved His faithfulness.

Trusting for others too!

It is one thing to trust the Lord for your personal finance but quite another thing to trust for someone else's. When Philip was asked to take over the Directorship of the *Centre Medical Evangélique* we knew that the centre was already in a debt situation which was getting worse month by month. This weighed heavily upon us. For several months Philip was accused of looking as though he was bearing all the Centre's burdens! But the Lord led him to victory and he could say, "Over to You, Lord! This is Your work, not mine." The situation was examined carefully. Some prudent measures were taken, and in six months we had our first monthly statement in the black. What rejoicing there was to find that the year-end statement was also in the black!

But the Lord had another lesson just around the corner. Nine months later there was a five-fold devaluation of the local currency, so that patients' receipts were only worth one-fifth of what they had been before. Prices had to go up to pay for medicines, and fewer people could afford to come to the hospital. We waited about six months to see how things would even out, but as the finances continued in the red a special commission was set up to study the situation. Before the commission met, the finances again reverted to the black. We have a total annual turnover of about one million US dollars. We are thankful that God owns the cattle on a thousand hills, and that He is faithful.

Points to Ponder:
1. Can you expect God to meet your financial needs if you do not tithe all that He gives you?
2. Have you proved the principle of 'creative' faith (i.e. trusting God to change something or someone; or to provide something or someone)?

Relevant scriptures:
1. Genesis 14:18-20, Malachi 3:8-10.
2. Luke 7:1-9, Luke 8:43-48.

17

STANDING AND MOVING IN FAITH

Matt and Margaret Paton

Taking it by faith

It was over the space of a few months — perhaps a year — that God dealt with us, teaching us vital principles that have remained with us over our years in central France.

In the small, fourth century town of Gannat, the little group of believers progressed to the point where it had outgrown the available space in our kitchen. Matt did the rounds, approaching every landlord who had property that looked capable of being made into a gospel meeting room. But it was not until God spoke to us through a former drug addict that the real adventure began. His word to us was, "Buy!"

Several times it seemed we were led to go down a particular road, and eventually Matt found in it an old house for sale. It was thought to be about 400 years old, and was badly in need of repair, including a new roof. Even though the price is low, how does that help you when you have just enough to buy necessary food and pay the rent to the end of the month?

The leaders of our missionary team approved of the project, but agreed that there was no money available for it, so we knew we had a faith battle ahead of us.

We set to, praying, believing, claiming and trusting. This went on for a month. We set aside times during the day, and sometimes at night, for waiting on the Lord.

During the succeeding month a gift arrived which exactly covered the cost of the house. Then another gift came in, exactly covering the cost of the roof repair, which was almost as much as the cost of the house.

Never, before or since, have we needed or received two such large amounts of money at almost the same time. So we have gone on, proving the Lord for His supply in material things.

While the big effort went on transforming the old building into a suitable meeting place and a residential flat for us, we held children's meetings in the town square. This, too, was an adventure of faith and we have no doubt that the thirty or so children who gathered with us will always remember what happened.

At that time all schools in France closed on a Thursday, so the children's meeting was held from March to September each Thursday afternoon. We trusted the Lord to give us dry weather every Thursday afternoon — and never were we disappointed!

In September the day off was changed from Thursday to Wednesday. We remarked to the children that perhaps it would rain next Thursday! Sure enough, the children were impressed with the fact that it poured the following Thursday. Our meeting on the Wednesday took place in dry weather as usual!

Handing over and moving on

The group in Gannat developed to the point

where it obviously needed French leadership. We realised our time there was over and that God had a fresh challenge for us. The pastor in another town asked us to open, with his help, a gospel work in Le Puy (the 'Lourdes' of the Middle Ages) and we agreed to go.

It was a dark place, still steeped in a medieval kind of Catholicism. We learned that four groups of Christians had tried to start a work there and had moved on in failure after a short time. It looked as if our failure would be the fifth, because the enemy seemed to be let loose to thwart the beginning of a Christian witness in that difficult place.

There was the strange accident to one of our boys; a deep sense of oppression; warnings of "terrible things to come", from a woman we contacted. The local priest warned his congregation about us.

What does one do in a situation like that? One Saturday we went off and climbed a hill. There we spent the day praising and proclaiming the name and power of Jesus over all the forces of darkness.

From that time, we continued to stand in faith, but without any particular feelings of victory or elation. Then God began to work. The enemy recoiled and people began to find the Lord. Even some nuns met the Lord, and one was later baptised and healed of near-blindness. Today a company of God's people thrives in that town under French leadership.

So we grew in an understanding of spiritual warfare.

Endurance and encouragement

Later, while in the midst of a busy life in

another industrial town, the Lord laid on Margaret's heart the need of the people in the high rise flats. Maybe knocking at doors, selling gospels, trying to converse with strangers, does not need the courageous faith of those who tramp through African or Indonesian forests. But it does require a particularly mature kind of faith to believe that behind those dirty doors, and at the top of those unhygienic stairs, are people prepared to receive a little Gospel of Mark into their hands, and later into their hearts.

It is also a challenge to be willing to go on in middle age doing with enthusiasm what one has been doing for twenty years. How often the enemy has arranged for the very first door to be slammed in our faces, with uncomplimentary remarks coming from the tenant!

We have also had to face the challenge of whether we could continue working among children and young people, but the following story encouraged us to do so.

Nineteen years ago Matt helped in a children's camp. A girl of ten who was there heard the gospel. Long years passed and in a different part of France, away in the mountainous region of Auvergne, Margaret began a children's meeting. Two little girls came along, learned the choruses, and then sang them in their tiny village after the meeting on Saturday evenings. They also repeated the Bible verses they had learned.

Memories flooded back into their mother's mind. She remembered how, years before, she had learned the same choruses and Bible verses. Tears flowed when she discovered that Matt was the husband of her children's Bible club leader.

We visited her, and the seed sown all those years before bore fruit. The mother came back to the Lord and now, together with her husband who has become a Christian, they witness with their daughters in their village.

Which way, Lord?

We have learned precious lessons in guidance, too. Once we were asked to take up residence in a particularly cold area. This was not a pleasant prospect for someone who feels the cold on a summer's day. On the morning of the day when the final decision had to be made, the reading included Proverbs 31:21, "When it snows, she has no fear."

We also proved God in the provision of a house in this new area. We had a very limited time in which to finalise arrangements. Where to start? We spent one day making fruitless enquiries at agencies. Could God drive the car and show us where to go?

We drove a short distance from the town centre and stopped. Leaving the car, we went to the mayor's office to enquire if there were any houses to let. Meanwhile, a Christian lady who had accompanied us walked a little way and enquired of a passer-by if he knew of any houses that were available. He said, "Certainly, follow me," and led the way back to our car. It was parked outside the only house in the whole town available for letting at that time! Within half an hour the formalities with the owner were over, and we had paid the first instalment of our rent. God had driven the car!

Points to Ponder:
1. "My God will meet all your needs according to His glorious riches in Christ Jesus." Are you proving this truth?
2. Are you able to recognise satanic activity? Is there a situation in which you should praise and proclaim the name and power of Jesus over the forces of darkness?

Relevant scriptures:
1. Philippians 4:19, Luke 10:1-8.
2. 2 Corinthians 11:14-15, 1 Peter 5:7-8.

SECTION 5

TRUST UNDER TRIAL

18

SING A SONG IN SINGAPORE

Maurice Charman

First steps in obedience

Ever since my conversion, which took place in March 1960, I have been aware that God has been the master planner behind my circumstances. He has moved me on in spiritual growth, in the forms of Christian service, and in the quality of that service to the body of Christ.

Moving on with God is not always easy. Over the years there have been some tough decisions to make and at times I have cried, "Enough! Enough!" But the Lord is patient, and when necessary has allowed extra time for deeper dealings which, in the end, have produced the right attitudes and decisions. Perhaps I am a poor student, but many of the lessons supposedly learned have had to be relearned.

When I was a very young Christian, the Lord somehow accommodated Himself to my restricted understanding of guidance and clearly led me to the WEC Missionary Training College in Tasmania. Towards the end of my training He just as clearly led me into WEC and showed me that I should go to Taiwan. At that time this was contrary to the views of some in the mission, so there were struggles. But I had a sincere willingness and desire to do only what was right, and in an amazing way the Lord proved to me the strength of 'fellowship'. Where there had been doubts in the minds of some, they were removed and I was accepted into WEC for ministry in Taiwan.

Waiting for God's time

After seven years in Taiwan I had a clear sense that my ministry there was finishing. But my own plans after that did not materialise. The lesson I had to learn then was that of trusting when I could not see. I understood God's plan after I had left Taiwan, as it was then that I married my wife, Ruth — the fulfilment of a promise given to me seven years before, when I was a missionary candidate! Through it all, I learned patience; in God's Kingdom there is no rush. I learned trust; what He has promised He not only gives, but does it without frenzied manoeuvring on our part.

Early in our marriage Ruth and I learned the truth of Isaiah 1:19, "If you are willing and obedient, you will eat the best from the land." We soon discovered that stated willingness without obedience is nothing. We had to obey, and to obey at that time was a commitment to a plan for the housing and discipling of overseas students.

In a joint venture between WEC and our local church we rented a five-bedroom house from one of our church deacons. When this proved too small we rented an eleven-bedroom house in one of Auckland's elite suburbs, and continued our hostel ministry there. During nearly four years this work was confirmed as right time and time again. It also proved to be the foundation and preparation for a later form of service.

Preparing for change

During 1978 there were distinct stirrings in our hearts. We sensed that the Lord was saying, "Prepare for change." Both Ruth and I knew that it would mean a move to Singapore. Initial reaction to our proposal was mixed, but in the Lord's timing I was asked to join Ken Booth, WEC's leader in Australia, for a visit to Singapore to carry out a survey and report on Asian missionary potential there. As a result of that report, Ruth and I were requested by our International leadership to establish a base for representation and missionary challenge.

We learned some good lessons while waiting interminably in New Zealand for our Singapore visas. In the end we decided to fix a date and trust the Lord that everything would be in order by that time. A day or two before our deadline there were still no visas, no available reservations on a flight, and virtually no money! I decided to phone Singapore and ask about our application. As soon as I was connected to the lawyer he said, with some amazement, that only that very day he had been advised that our visas had been granted! My next call was to our travel agent who, with similar amazement, told us that he had only just received a telex telling him of four available seats on the flight we wanted. To complete the story, the day before our departure all the money needed was in hand. Praise the Lord!

The move contested

We arrived in Singapore in November 1980 and right from the commencement experienced intense opposition.

After only a couple of days our son Daniel, then aged four, slipped on wet concrete and had to spend a night in the Singapore General Hospital with delayed concussion. A few days afterwards he developed an allergy, something he had never had before. It took a long course of antihistamines to sort out that problem. Later he was climbing a brick wall in the place where we were staying and pulled himself up by hanging on to an un-cemented ornamental brick. He fell quite a distance with the brick hitting the back of his head. He was brought in to us screaming, and with blood flowing from his head. The doctor allowed us to keep him at home overnight and the next morning he was fine.

That day we were taken to the zoo for an outing with some friends. Only a few minutes after we had commenced our trip the back door of the small mini bus flew open and our six-year-old daughter was thrown out into one of Singapore's busiest roads at rush hour. Fortunately she had the presence of mind to pick herself up and run to the side of the road. When we were able to collect her from there, the length of her back was bruised, but that was all!

In our case this was not the straw that broke the camel's back, but the excess that helped us recognise who was behind all the calamities. The enemy had gone too far. We dealt with him by using the authority of the Name of Jesus. It would have been easy for us to give in, but that excess was what we needed to strengthen our resolve, and in so doing we were able to deal with the situation in the right way.

Continuing pressures

Pressure still comes from many different quar-

ters. We have had the problems of schooling to
cope with, as well as the problem of housing in a
city of high living costs.

For eighteen months we lived in an apartment,
one of sixteen in a block set near the main road.
We were the only Christians in the whole block
and all our neighbours were ardent Buddhists or
Taoists. Over the wall we had the continuous
backdrop of a Buddhist medium, gonging and
bonging at all hours of the day and night.

With the arrival of new missionaries we needed
a larger house. Knowing that this involved a
major decision, we approached it with prayer and
fasting. We were led to the passage in the Bible
where King Jehoshophat led his people up the
mountain against a vast enemy army. As they
marched up the mountain they praised God, em-
phasising two basic aspects of His character, His
love and His holiness. The word to us that day was
that we should identify our problem (housing),
and sing to it, believing that what seemed a mountain could under the hand of God become nothing. It seemed 'far out', but that is what we did.

In our time of prayer we had been joined by a
visitor from our church in New Zealand. As we
concluded our meeting, he shared with us an
impression he had had from the Lord. He said
that a house would be provided for us through
the agency of two men whom we knew.

On the day that we were due to renew the con-
tract on our old house, we had a phone call from a
friend. He told us of the possibility of a house. We
went to look at it and made the unanimous decision that we should take it. When the landlord
of the new place rang up to see what we thought
of it, I recognised his voice. Yes, he was the second

of the two men that we would know! So God helped us surmount the obstacle of housing in Singapore and, through having an established relationship, the new house was offered to us at very favourable terms.

We have had our problems with visas as well, but on two occasions we have seen the Lord miraculously intervene on our behalf when the situation appeared hopeless. The twelve months from mid-1984 were the most difficult we have ever had. I had major surgery for a burst appendix, followed by three return trips to hospital, twice in Britain and once in Singapore. Our son Daniel had his own health problems, and in the same period there were three family deaths. We feel more able to relate to the experiences of Job! Like him, although we do not fully understand why so much has gone wrong, we have the faith to believe that He who has led us thus far, will also lead us out and on.

Certainly there have been positive results in spite of the difficulties. We have a functioning Board that is very supportive of us and our ministry. The Board is made up of people I met when in Singapore for the exploratory visit in 1979. From those early, preliminary contacts the Lord put us in touch with people who wished to join us. So far we have seen three young people going to missionary work overseas — one each to Taiwan, Pakistan and Sri Lanka. A steady stream of young people are going to the Missionary Training College in Tasmania, and we are currently interviewing and counselling others who have the mission field, or training for it, in mind. Opportunities to minister in churches abound, and it is through these that much of the response is coming.

Points to Ponder:
1. Are you trusting the Lord where you cannot 'see', and expecting Him to do what He has promised?
2. How does one recognise whether a problem or pressure is from God or from the devil?

Relevant scriptures:
1. Psalm 37:1-7.
2. 2 Corinthians 10:1-5, 1 John 4:1-6.

19

LEARNING THE LORD'S LESSONS

Cecily Booth

A contented missionary kid

As she prayed, a young South African woman saw before her a map traversed by a huge river. As she watched, one bend in the river became magnified and she saw a crowd of brown-skinned people kneeling with hands raised. "Come over and help us," they cried. An examination of a map confirmed that Dulcie Sheasby had seen a bend in the River Ganges on the Indian subcontinent. It is not surprising that a short time later she was on her way to that place as a missionary. There she met and married an English clergyman, Frank Martin.

So I was born in a godly missionary home. I spoke Hindi before I spoke English. From an early age I heard people being told to "give their hearts to Jesus", and when I was eight years old I did that at my mother's knee. I had the very real pleasure of living in a boarding school for 'missionary kids'.

Through my teen years I found myself looking sideways at the worldly excitements that were so attractive, and so forbidden! When I was eighteen I faced up to the question of who was to be boss of my life. I had exciting plans for myself, but suddenly I found that I wanted God's plans more than mine. Within six weeks I was in Bible School in England preparing for the mission field.

A lesson in submission

"Sit down, dear." I was having my second term interview with our Bible School Principal. I had been so immature the first term that things had gone badly, but they had been so much better in the second that I mentally 'polished my badge', thinking I had done rather well. It would be nice to be commended.

"You know, dear, you really don't like gardening, do you?" (Whatever gave her that idea?) "When you come with the others to my drawing room you should sit on the floor and leave the seats for older people." (Hadn't she noticed that I had been doing that all this term?) "It really is bad manners to go out into the kitchen and scrape the crusty bits of cheese off the pans." I was shattered! Somewhat rebelliously, that night I asked the Lord all about it. "Lord, you know that was all to do with last term! I am doing so well this term. Didn't she see the difference?" Then I seemed to hear Him say, "Accept it and learn from it. What about the things she could have said if she really knew your heart?" I replied, "Yes, Lord. Your hammer always hits the nail on the head!"

God's call to the Tibetan Border and WEC moved me back to India in 1951. The day I left England, a young Australian, Ken Booth, later to become my husband, landed in India. We were married in 1955 and in 1956 were elected to leadership of WEC's Himalayan field, as it was then known.

A lesson in healing

Oh, those poor Tibetan refugees! Hundreds of them, several times a week, were coming to our door for food relief. What an opportunity to reach these people from a closed land with the news that Someone cared enough to send us to help them; but more than that, to send His Son for them. Coming from altitudes of thirteen thousand feet to India, sickness had caught up with many of them. Through constant contact with them, Ken fell sick with a lung infection which the doctor diagnosed as tuberculosis. Now who was to keep the relief programme going and run the field? For nine months Ken continued to manage both from his bed, but he got steadily worse. (It turned out that he was allergic to streptomycin.)

Several of us gathered upstairs for the WEC prayer meeting and suddenly one spoke up, "I think we should go down, lay hands on Ken and anoint him with oil." There were nods of assent, but some felt that, according to Scripture, Ken must request it first himself. At this juncture there was a break, and I took Ken his cup of tea. As I entered the door he said, "Will you ask the folks to come down and lay hands on me?" There was such a sense of the power and presence of God in that room as we prayed that we hardly needed the X-ray a fortnight later to show that he had been healed.

A lesson in God's higher ways

Healed? Of the lung condition, yes. But what a heavy year it had been! Ken's nine months of illness and the refugee relief programme had demanded so much from us. It became obvious that we ought to go home on sick leave for a while, but there were no passages available on the ships that passed through Bombay. We had to wait in Lucknow, which was twenty-four hours' train journey from Bombay. There was not much hope for last minute cancellations, and in any case we couldn't afford a hotel in Bombay.

While in Lucknow, slowly and patiently, Ian, aged five, had made friends with a big white alsatian which tended to be nervous and uncertain with children. It was Rex's supper time. Ian knelt down before him and trustingly put his arms round the dog's neck. Suddenly there was a snapping and a scream. We rushed in to find that Rex had panicked and bitten Ian in the face twice. His face was covered with blood and his nose and lip were bitten right through.

My thoughts were in a whirl as we rushed him to the hospital. "Lord, why this? And why now, when it seems to be more than we can handle?" Then came the assurance, "My thoughts are higher than your thoughts."

The next day I spotted what I thought was a familiar figure crossing the courtyard of the hospital and called out to her. It wasn't who I thought it was, but calling out to her was to prove no mistake! "You are the lady whose little boy has been bitten by a dog," she said. "Why are you here in Lucknow?" I explained our dilemma and the problem of getting a last-minute passage because of being unable to wait in Bombay. "That's no problem," was her reply. "I'm from Bombay and I can give you the address of a mission bungalow where you can stay and look after yourselves, and be available to get on the ship as soon as a passage is offered."

"Thank you, Lord! Your ways are so much higher than ours. You take our 'too much' and turn it into a beautiful answer to prayer."

A lesson in humility

After all his experiences Ken was suffering from nervous exhaustion. Somehow the nervous illness got worse on arrival in Australia, and the whole burden of our little family fell on me. It was at this time, when we seemed to be scraping the bottom of the barrel nervously, that I received 'The Letter'. Someone, meaning well, wrote to tell me all the things that I was doing wrong. "Ken is sick because of you. We want you back on the field, but not unless you are different." I crawled away into a mental hole to lick my wounds.

"Lord, is it true? Is it really as bad as that?" I sobbed. It seemed just the last straw, at the wrong time. My mind ran hither and thither looking for escape. I even contemplated trying to make arrangements for my family and then leaving them, since I was such a bad influence. Gently the Lord seemed to be bringing me back to something. Was He trying to speak or wasn't He? Was I too busy flailing around to hear? Then I knew. "Lord, You'll have to do something new for me or I can't go on. It's like that time at Bible School, isn't it? I may not be as bad as what was written in The Letter, but I do need Your touch, Lord. And there is a basis of truth in what was written." Waves of Love flooded through me. Suddenly it didn't matter any more that I wasn't much good. I had had such an out**pouring** of Himself that I could once again face **tomorr**ow.

Lessons about finance

From early to more recent days, the Lord has had to chivy us about trusting Him completely.

I well remember a time of severe and continuing financial shortage early in our marriage in

India. Our allowances covered our food bills, but there were other needs. The months passed and it was time for the birth of our first baby. There wasn't even the money for a taxi, so I walked into hospital in labour and used the equipment provided for the poor Nepalis. "Lord, is this right? We can't even buy toothpaste because we know there is a medical bill coming up tomorrow." Suddenly it was as if something snapped. "Lord, I'm not going on like this! We are Your ambassadors, and earthly ambassadors never have to worry about where their supplies are coming from; they don't even have to ask. I'm going to buy toothpaste today if I need it, and You will have to look after the bill tomorrow. If You don't, it will be to Your discredit, not ours." I laughed out loud! Release! And the money did come, and the medical bill was paid. From then on our needs were met.

When we had been back in Australia for three years due to Ken's illness, we were comfortably settled. Then it became uncomfortable because we had a nagging feeling that God was pushing us out to India again. "Well, Lord, we haven't got the 'No objection to return' stamped in our passports so, humanly speaking, it's impossible. But if You want us to go You can provide the visas." I was fairly smug for I didn't think that was likely. A few weeks later the phone rang, "Just to let you know that your visas are through!" Gasp! Now the problem was finance.

I said to Ken, "Let's keep the car till the last minute. The Lord will supply our fares and when we sell the car we'll have all the money required for customs and travel within India." Sensible surely! But somehow, nothing moved. The days passed and no money came. Not only that, there was something just a little uncomfortable in our relationship with the Lord.

At last it was clear what we had to do. "Okay, Lord, You can have the car for our fares, even if we have to go to India without anything in hand to cover expenses at the other end." We still couldn't see how it was going to work out but the peace of God guarded our minds and thoughts. To our utter amazement the car didn't sell! However, the money started to come in and by the time we came to leave, our fares were covered and we had the car money in hand.

Lessons about daily living

We were seated on the floor in the little meeting hall, men on one side, women on the other. It was hot and the fans were gently turning, stirring the warm air. The Nigerian brother had a shining face and it was more than perspiration. He was opening up his heart. "Brothers and sisters, I want to talk to you about the 'Thieves of our Todays'. There are two thieves that all the time want to try and steal our todays. One is Mr Yesterday, with his regrets about what happened, and the other is Mr Tomorrow who endlessly mulls round and round our problems. So we always end up with yesterday or tomorrow and we never have the full use of today." I needed that! I know all about my thoughts going round and round.

But there is another thief whose main task is to attack the Lord's servants, especially those in positions of leadership, Mr Too Busy. It happened a few years ago in Australia. Ken and I were fully occupied. There was always someone to see, some letter to write, something to organise. We discovered that a coldness had crept into our relationship. Little things about each other tended to irritate. We still loved each other and our relationship was good, but we had lost out on personal communication, and the one who had stolen it was Mr Too Busy. Soon after that the fellowship felt we should have an extended break for health reasons. Gradually we re-established three levels of communication: simple sharing, willingness to trace back little irritations to the incident which was the source, and finally opening up our hearts to each other in depth, sharing our hopes, visions and dreams. It took several weeks to come round to being just 'us' together again.

Recently the Lord has been trusting us with something of the mystery of the unexplained, things we don't understand now but which we will know in His tomorrow. We live day by day, praying that we will not allow ourselves to be robbed by Mr Yesterday or Mr Tomorrow or Mr Too Busy.

Points to Ponder:
1. How do you handle criticism, especially if unjustified? What place should prayer have in this?
2. Are you really *living* today, or are regrets, busyness and anxiety robbing you of today's blessings?

Relevant scriptures:
1. Isaiah 53:6, Matthew 5:11-12.
2. Psalm 103, Matthew 6:25-34.

20

MIDDLE EAST MARATHON

'Alex McFarlane'
(Proper names have been altered
in the interests of security.)

A concert pianist?

They tell me I was born in Minneapolis, Minnesota, in the summer of 1949, but I don't remember much about the incident. At any rate, we soon left there and eventually settled in Cincinnati, Ohio, where I enjoyed all the advantages of growing up in a Christian home, with good teaching and lots of encouragement. At the age of seven I made a personal commitment to follow Christ.

It was about that same time that I began to take piano lessons, which continued for the next eight or nine years. I loved the piano, although I occasionally balked at the practice hours. During my high school years I became involved in church activities and Youth For Christ, singing and playing the piano in various musical groups. Somehow, my memories of those years include almost nothing in the way of schoolwork.

People were very encouraging concerning my talent on the piano. "That's great," they would say. "Develop that gift and God can use it. He can do great things with a talent like that!" I may have entertained lofty visions of performing before great crowds who, overcome by the majesty of the music, would come streaming to Christ.

But at some point along the way I realised that God didn't particularly need a piano. He could, if He so desired, create pianos (and piano players) out of the rocks by the roadside. What He wanted was not my talent, but me. The only thing I had to offer Him was my life, free from the clutter of things I may have thought valuable. It was up to Him to do with the accessories as He pleased.

A lifetime task?

As high school graduation neared I was compelled to do some serious thinking about the future. I had always enjoyed mathematics and had considered pursuing a career in engineering. But in the back of my mind was the thought of the foreign mission field, the fruit of seeds planted during my earliest days in church. As the Lord seemed to confirm this interest, I applied to Prairie Bible Institute in Western Canada and headed off to Bible school in the autumn of 1967.

The classes were challenging, the teaching excellent, but what the Lord used more than anything to provide guidance for the future was the programme of daily missionary prayer groups, each praying for a different area of the globe. My first year I spent as a prayer group tramp, wandering from group to group, not at all certain where God wanted me. During my second year I gravitated into what was called the Central Asia prayer group, which covered everywhere from the Middle East to India. What struck me hardest was the fact that many of these predominately Muslim countries were virtually untouched by the gospel.

Gradually the Lord narrowed the range until one particular country came into focus. A term paper for a senior missions class was another factor in my growing interest in 'Clumbe', ninety-nine percent Muslim, with hardly any evangelical witness. As the country became clear, I looked around for a mission society working in the area. Considering that Prairie Bible Institute was regularly invaded during semi-annual missionary conferences by more than 100 missionary societies, it was surprisingly difficult to find one even interested in an outreach to Clumbe. Eventually I discovered WEC. Doing another term paper in the same missions class helped to confirm that leading, and by the time graduation day arrived I had already sent in my preliminary application.

The autumn of 1970 saw me off to WEC's six-month Candidate Course. In addition to the routine of classes and lectures, I had the privilege of being introduced to many activities about which I knew absolutely nothing, such as electrical wiring, office construction and cooking breakfast with a roommate who was equally ignorant!

A life partner?

During this time an extracurricular interest was developing, involving a fellow Prairie graduate from Idaho. We continued to correspond and after I was accepted into WEC in February I headed west with a team to visit various Bible schools in the Canadian prairies. During a week-long stay at Prairie 'Sue' and I were engaged — conditionally. Obviously I was quite sure that the Lord had led me into WEC and was leading me to Clumbe, so it seemed logical that if He wanted us to spend our lives together He would lead Sue in the same way. Besides, I was quite certain that if they had accepted somebody like me, Sue would be a 'shoo-in'.

While Sue began her time as a candidate the following autumn, I headed off to the promised land. I was twenty-two years old, naive and inexperienced. I'm sure that if I had been the field leader in those days I would have been scared to death of me. Fortunately there was no field leader to entertain such thoughts. In fact, there was really no field, only a scattering of perhaps twenty-five workers throughout the country from a variety of groups and backgrounds.

Probably the most valuable gift I received that year from the Lord was a deep love for the Clumbian language and, through that, an intense desire to identify with the Clumbian people. It is relatively easy to proclaim a sentimental love for a people one has never met, and who are an ocean away. But to be honest, I had often felt like Charlie Brown, who once said, "I love humanity; it's people I can't stand!" Being friendly was fine, but getting close to people was dangerous; one could get hurt that way. Yet I realised that there was no way I could do the job the Lord had sent me to do without becoming intimately involved in the lives of people.

The following summer Sue and I were married in Idaho and six weeks later returned together to the capital of Clumbe. While looking for a house of our own, we lived with a Finnish family. They were Lutherans, people who baptised babies and held other such beliefs that I had been taught were unscriptural! And yet they were so obviously part of the same family, so evidently of the same Spirit. We learned in those early years to value greatly the fellowship of our brothers and sisters, no matter what minor differences in doctrine and practice might be present. The fact that there were so few of us was a blessing in disguise. We did not have the luxury of choosing from a great multitude of believers the ones we would deign to fellowship with. We had no choice but to accept what was available, and we have been greatly blessed because of it.

Can Muslims really be saved?

We soon became acquainted with the tensions of working among an unresponsive people. There were very few ethnic Clumbian believers, and of those who had made some sort of 'decision', many had since fallen away. There seemed to be considerable evidence to support the claim of those who said that a Muslim could not really be saved.

A good part of the tension stemmed from the expectation of Christians in the West, and what seemed sometimes to be a 'head-hunting' mentality in evangelism. I had vivid memories of a summer spent during Bible school, working with children's clubs in Michigan. We would go to an assigned area for a week of Bible teaching, rounding up whatever children we could find in the neighbourhood. Since most of the workers were girls, we fellows were assigned to the clubs in tough areas of the large cities where sometimes nearly a hundred children would gather. At the end of each lesson we would give an invitation to those who wanted to give their lives to Jesus. A good presentation would almost always get a good response. It was obvious that many who came forward were simply playing follow-the-leader. But not having the infinite wisdom necessary to discern all hearts, we would pray with all who came and dutifully mark their decision on an attendance sheet.

At the end of eight weeks, a final rally was held for all the summer workers and their parents. We were introduced one by one, with statistics recited concerning attendance and conversions. About halfway through the presentations I realised what was happening. The introductions were being made according to the number of recorded conversions, lowest to highest. The clear implication was that those with more converts were superior workers. Having had some of the largest clubs I was in first place, but I was keenly aware of the unfairness of the evaluation.

Clumbians were not exactly breaking down the walls to hear the gospel. Converts from Islam were rare, those who lasted more than a year or two were very rare. Yet we were convinced that we were in the place where the Lord wanted us. We had to learn what it means to run a marathon, not a one-hundred-metre dash.

People or projects?

I became involved in translating, literature production, and the preparation of a modern Clumbian version of the New Testament. Since there was so little available, every additional tool was a cause for rejoicing. For several years progress was steady. However, the Enemy has recently intensified his opposition to such projects, as we have seen books banned, believers harassed with court proceedings, and the sale of the Bible restricted.

All of these literature efforts have been projects which afforded some sense of accomplishment, with visible milestones of progress. Yet the primary concern is still people, not projects. How does one measure progress? The statistics would indicate that Clumbe is a country where the number of believers, including Muslim converts, has increased by four or five hundred percent over the past fifteen years. The same statistics would show that Clumbe is a country with perhaps one believer for every 50,000 to 100,000 people, with half-a-dozen struggling fellowships in the entire land.

There is obviously much work to be done, and we must press on with the task at hand. Our motivation must also be obvious. It is not the responsiveness of the hearers or the great sense of fulfilment we receive in sharing, but our obedience to the Lord's commands and His constraining love.

Points to Ponder:

1. Do you distance yourself from others, or do you become involved despite the possibility of being hurt?

2. Does your sense of fulfilment come from having achieved recognisable goals, or from a deep assurance that you have done the will of God?

Relevant scriptures.

1. Luke 10:33-36, 1 Thessalonians 2:7-12, 2 Corinthians 4:3-6.

2. John 4:34, 1 John 2:17.

21

PAPER MISSIONARY

Geoff McEvansoneya

Latching on to literature

Although I had been converted earlier, it was not until after my baptism at eleven that the Lord began to be very real and personal to me. In the Brethren church where I was brought up the folk certainly knew their Bible, and taught it. At secondary school, it was not long before others realised that in at least one respect I was rather odd — yet this gave opportunities for witness, as well as a standard to live up to.

When I was fifteen, I wanted to earn some money during the school summer holidays, and got a job selling refreshments at the local railway station, mainly to holiday-makers when the packed trains stopped. The following summer I was looking forward to doing this again, when I heard of the sudden death of the owner of the station cafeteria and the consequent closure of the business. I was at a loss to know what to do for the coming weeks.

Then I remembered a friend of our family, Sid Latham, who with his wife Pauline ran a small Christian printing works in a nearby town. Starting with a very small hand press, he had built the work up, eventually leaving his trade and taking work as a part-time postman, so that he could give five or six hours a day to printing Christian literature. He had moved from an old chicken coop, via a rather dilapidated shed, to the luxury of the town's old steamroller shed.

Sid and Pauline are a couple full of faith and zeal for the Lord, and the work has expanded so much that it is now one of the largest Christian printing enterprises in the whole country.

Back in 1966, with a growing demand, they had been praying for someone who could assist them over the summer period. Not knowing this, I asked them if I could help, and was thrilled when they told me I was an answer to prayer.

What was meant to be five weeks eventually became more than seven years of helping in the work of the Gospel Press — at least during school holidays and subsequently university and college vacations. I enjoyed my time at university, but it was so much more exciting to come home and be involved five months a year in helping to print Christian, mainly evangelistic, literature.

Towards the end of my College course I met Angela, and God confirmed that He wanted us to serve Him together.

Battle for our baby

Student days came to an end. The Lord led me into teaching. That involved not only moving to the London area but severing the ties I had had with Christian printing. Angela and I were married in 1973 and went to live in Haslemere in Surrey, where we joined the Evangelical Church. Only seven years old, it was a growing, loving fellowship in which we were very happy.

The degree of love and concern was soon shown to us in the months following the birth of our first child, Ian, in 1974. Born with a gap in his intestines, his life hung by a thread for three months of desperate illness which involved three operations in the Great Ormond Street Hospital. The whole church stood with us both practically and in prayer. The night that two-days-old Ian was rushed from Guildford to Great Ormond Street for an emergency operation, I left the hospital shattered by all that was happening. I had just signed consent forms for the operation to save his life, and as I left Haslemere station, I spotted Tom, the pastor of our church, and another friend, Rita, who had come to meet me. Neither knew the other would be there. We went around to Rita's house where she, her husband Jim, and Tom went on their knees with me and prayed to the Saviour to take care of this little baby and to see him through all that lay ahead. Tom spent sleepless nights praying for Ian, and it was a great encouragement to hear a word that the Lord had given him as dawn broke one morning, 'This sickness shall not be unto death.'

The weeks went by and Ian could only be fed intravenously. Any milk given to him by mouth just wouldn't stay down. Further operations ensued. Then one night the whole church had a special prayer meeting. The next day he kept food down for the first time!

It was a time when the Lord taught us our utter dependence on Him. It was also a time of learning for the church, because it was the first time it had been faced with the serious illness of a young child.

The printed page again

I found my teaching and our church involvement fulfilling, yet at the same time I missed the work of the Gospel Press, and felt that the Lord still wanted to use me in literature work.

Then, early in 1976, I received a letter out of the blue from Tony Whittaker, whom I had known as a fellow student at Bristol University years before. I had not known Tony that well, in fact I had to think which Tony it was! In the letter, he spoke of having recently moved with his family to work at the headquarters of *SOON*, the gospel broadsheet ministry of WEC International.

In replying, I asked Tony what *SOON* was, how it operated, and how one could help? Perhaps this was how the Lord intended my experience and interest in printing to be used? Within a few weeks, both Angela and I had become very much involved in the work, helping to dispatch the *SOON* broadsheets, marking Bible courses, typing address labels and acting as pen friends to a contact in Poland.

We found the work really exciting, not just doing it, but knowing the Lord was using us to be a blessing to many others. We were missionaries from our own house. The work grew on us and took up an increasing amount of our spare time. Within a few months I began to wonder whether the Lord might actually be calling us into full-time work with *SOON*.

I mentioned this feeling to Angela, but it was clearly one which she did not and could not share. Full-time work, very possibly overseas work, but not in an office! Whilst I knew God had given me administrative gifts, Angela felt her's lay more in personal work. I could only think I had made a mistake. So, for the time being at least, I was to remain in teaching, and *SOON* was to be a spare-time activity.

The years passed until, in early 1979, we felt sure that the time for stepping out into full-time work was imminent. What kind of work was, however, a mystery! Then in September two important things happened. Early in the month, we went to stay for a weekend at the *SOON* headquarters at Willington, near Derby. I could not be there without again wanting to be more involved, but I knew that the call was one which Angela did not share.

SOON call — Scripture confirmation

At the end of the month, I went to the Annual *SOON* Reunion at Bolney, Sussex, *SOON's* base for many years before the move to Willington. During that meeting the Lord spoke very clearly. John and Nellie Lewis talked about the need of more full-time workers for Gospel Literature Worldwide. Nellie said, "We older ones are getting on," and that the future would be in the hands of the "younger ones like Tony... and Geoff". I almost fell off my seat, but told myself that she had only mentioned me because I was one of the younger ones in the meeting. But the Lord told me that that was not what He had meant.

I went home to Angela who had not been able to come to the meeting. When I shared with her how the Lord had spoken, she then gave me the second shock of the day. She told me that during that very evening she had had a clear call to the *SOON* work! Different place, different circumstances, but as clear a call as I had had.

Shortly afterwards, the Lord confirmed this from Scripture. In Psalm 107:4-7 (Good News Bible) I read, "Some wandered in the trackless desert and could not find their way to a city to live in. They were hungry and thirsty and had given up all hope. Then in their trouble they called to the Lord, and He saved them from their distress. He led them by a straight road to a city where they could live." The summer of 1979 had been like a trackless desert to us: we were depressed, we could not see where we were going. The Lord answered our prayer — His service through *SOON* was to be the "city where we could live".

The story does not end there. Visits to the WEC headquarters followed; interviews and more interviews with members of the Candidate Committee; months of waiting and looking for the post each morning, and eventually acceptance for the Candidate Course.

We were accepted into WEC at the end of the Candidate Course and in January 1981 joined the *SOON* work. The years since have been exciting as we have seen the work grow from a circulation of 360,000 copies each quarterly issue to a current figure of over 650,000, with responses pouring in at an ever-increasing rate (over 1700 per week) from all over the world.

Points to Ponder:
1. Is your church a loving, caring fellowship? What can you do to make it more so?
2. How would you describe your level of productivity for the kingdom of God? How could it be increased?

Relevant scriptures:
1. 1 John 4:7-21.
2. John 15:1-8.

22

FORTY-NINE YEARS OF MIRACLES

Frank Chapman

Trials and miracles

All through my Christian life the Lord has graciously dealt with me in one of two ways. Either He has allowed trials in which He has provided a way of escape in His perfect timing, or He has performed miracles to encourage my faith.

I dedicated my life to the Lord on 24 December 1937, promising that I would do anything He wanted me to do and go anywhere He sent me.

This resulted in my attending Prairie Bible Institute in Western Canada where I learned much about the need of the 'regions beyond'. Through Bible study, and by reading the life story of C.T. Studd, I became convinced that God wanted me on the mission field.

But where? A worker in the old CIM advised me to go to Colombia, since I was too old for China! Having already met a fine young lady who also wanted to serve the Lord in Colombia, it wasn't difficult for me to accept this as the Lord's leading.

But I had to serve in the Canadian army first. While on embarkation leave I presented Winnifred Wilson with an engagement ring, promising that I would marry her after the war. When it ended I returned to Canada and applied to WEC. By April 1946 Winnifred and I were two of nine candidates for Colombia taking the orientation course.

Visas for Colombia were hard to obtain. While we were all at a conference, our American leader, Alfred Ruscoe, called us together and challenged us, as a group, to trust God for them. There was no instant response from the others, but I stood up and thanked the Lord that He would release the visas within two months.

A week later we learned that someone had obtained a visa from the Colombian vice-consul in Galveston, Texas. Four candidates left immediately by train, and five others left by car, and in a few days we all had our visas.

Soon after, when Winnie was at our Philadelphia regional headquarters and I was at our Charlotte centre, an emergency arose in the tiny country of Spanish Guinea (now Equatorial Guinea) in West Africa. Mrs Thorne, wife of the field leader, had become very ill and had returned to Britain. Mr Thorne wrote asking British WEC to send out a young couple as soon as possible, and, as none was available, the British staff had appealed for help to the North American branch.

Circumstantial guidance

Our leaders met to discuss this, and in his inimitable way Mr Ruscoe suggested that if they didn't have a couple perhaps they could "make a couple"! They agreed that our marriage could be the solution to the problem — but what about our guidance to Colombia? It was decided that a staff member in Charlotte should discuss it with me and another with Winnie in Philadelphia. So one Saturday morning in November Mr Hancox asked me to pray about going to Spanish Guinea. This was a big challenge. However, that same night I had the answer. Following a Moody Bible Institute chart, I read Hebrews 13:7: "Remember your leaders, who spoke the word of God . . ." I knew immediately that that was God's word to me. I read on to the end of the chapter and found in verse seventeen, "Obey your leaders and submit to their authority."

The next day I wrote Winnifred telling her I wouldn't be going to Colombia but to Spanish Guinea. I wondered what her reaction would be. But a few days later I received her letter telling me that God must want us to serve Him together in Spanish Guinea, because He had already spoken to her about going to Spanish Guinea just before the staff had discussed it with her. After hearing about God's separate guidance to each of us, our leaders advised us to get married as soon as convenient. We were delighted to obey that instruction as well!

But we had further tests about our visas. It was necessary to appeal to Spain for permission to enter her colony of Spanish Guinea. Our first application was ignored and our second was rejected. However, God had called us, and on 4 March 1948, we sailed by freighter for Africa, having obtained a temporary visa for the adjacent territory of Cameroun. Mr Thorne had asked the local authorities a number of times for entry permits. While we were crossing the Atlantic, he appealed again and was given a favourable reply, enabling us to go right into the country.

God uses our baby boy

Several years later, in 1950, God called Evelyn Wilson (now Mrs Evelyn Geake) to join us. She too made her journey to the Cameroun on a temporary visa. On that occasion, Winnie and I, with six-month-old Jonathan, went to the coast to obtain permission for Evelyn's entry to Spanish Guinea. As I read God's word and prayed, 1 Corinthians 16:9 stood out, "A great door for effective work has opened to me." I knew then that God was going to provide.

We went to see the Governor, and as soon as he saw our baby boy he was elated. He had a son in Spain of about the same age, whom he had not yet seen. I took Jonathan from Winnie and handed him to the Governor. He was overjoyed, and walked around the office so proudly. I then informed him that this baby's auntie was on her way to assist us, and that I supposed it would be all right for her to come. He said "Yes, yes, yes." At the proper moment I retrieved our baby, thanked the Governor and went to the Cameroun to meet Evelyn. As we came to the Spanish Guinea border, the guards asked for Evelyn's visa. I assured them that I had the word of the Governor. Reluctantly they let her into the country. The Lord had used a baby boy to open a closed door.

The life of faith is challenging and sometimes positively exciting. We had to learn that God was able not only to guide us, and to provide visas, but to perform miracles on our behalf.

Healed of diabetes

In early 1957 I became afflicted with running abscesses on my legs and back. Injections of Terramycin relieved the condition but did not cure it. I grew worse, so we went to the Cameroun and I had thorough blood tests in two different hospitals. The verdict: my pancreas had ceased to function and I was diabetic. My doctor advised that I return to Canada, commence insulin treatment and adhere to a good diet, after which I may be able to return to Africa.

We prayed and asked the Lord to send a miracle gift of $2,000 for our travel, or else perform a miracle by healing my body. As I was reading Psalm 37 one morning, verse four challenged me. It says, "Delight yourself in the Lord and He will give you the desires of your heart." From then on we knew that God was going to heal. Rather than returning to Canada, we returned to our work. I did not take any insulin and I was unable to procure the special diet. I did not even cut out the use of sugar. As we settled down again, the abscesses cleared up on their own without medication.

After four weeks I went back to hospital and asked for another thorough blood test. Blood was taken periodically from my veins and I was asked to come back in the evening for the report. As I entered the laboratory, the technician smiled and informed me that my pancreas was functioning perfectly. "In fact," he said, "there is not another man in the country with better blood than yours!" Since 1957 I have had no diabetic problems. All praise be to the Lord!

What about many devoted servants of the Lord who are not healed of their diabetic condition? Are they failing to believe God for a miracle? Are they less spiritual? By no means; God has shown me that it takes more spirituality to live with diabetes than without it.

Roast leopard for lunch

In 1956, I was away on a trek lasting several

weeks. When I arrived home Winnie told me that we had a problem. Someone was stealing our chickens. She would hear a squawk at night, and next day another chicken would be missing. I told her to let me know when she heard the next squawk and I would see what could be done about it.

Around midnight on the second night she wakened me. Speed and quietness were essential. As I put on my robe and heavy slippers I heard the next squawk, so knew in which direction to go. Speeding across the compound, I flashed on my torch. Instead of finding an African, I saw the head of a young leopard with the rooster in his mouth! He had turned to see what was coming, and as I was in step I kicked him hard in the jaw, knocking him out. I then grabbed his tail, swung him in the air, and banged his head on the hard ground, killing him. We had roast chicken that day, and the Africans had roast leopard.

Personal renewal

The most rewarding experience that Winnie and I had was a deeper work of the Holy Spirit in our hearts. We had witnessed God's great power in guiding us, providing visas for us, healing us, and giving me strength to kill a leopard bare-handed, yet the Lord still had something vital to teach us.

After my healing in 1957, I was seeking the Lord in a special way. He showed me that I needed revival in my heart. I had allowed coldness to enter through my anti-charismatic position. The Holy Spirit convicted me of wrong attitudes towards my brothers of that persuasion. Thank the Lord that, on my humble confession, He forgave me, cleansed me from my sin, and gave me a 'baptism' of love for all men. God has given us greater joy, greater love, greater power in ministry and greater release in the Spirit.

Points to Ponder:
1. Can you submit to Christian leaders without hassles, or do you hold out for your own way?
2. What is the secret of loving people with whom you disagree?

Relevant scriptures:
1. Hebrews 13:7.
2. Galatians 5:22-26, 1 Corinthians 13.

SECTION 6

UNLIKELY CANDIDATES

23

NOT PLANNING TO QUIT, BUT EXPECTING TO REAP

Rita Egli

Nonstarter starts with God

Had you known me as a child, you would never have guessed that I would become a missionary. A broken home, a working mother, little parental supervision, too much 'freedom', and no gospel — hardly 'good missionary training'! Yet God was seeking me. Early on, I became aware of sin in my life, which I knew was not forgiven. When I was nine, a barmaid read the Bible to me on one or two occasions, and that set me searching. For the next few years, I visited various churches without finding an answer for my unsettled conscience. "Be good . . . Be like Jesus". Such pious platitudes inspired no hope in me. I couldn't do it. I had already failed.

One night, at the age of thirteen I was in a meeting when I finally grasped the good news: Jesus had died for the sins of the world. That included *my* sins, those sins that had been plaguing my conscience for so long. That night I came to Him and He received me. My conscience was as clear as if I'd never sinned. A new life had begun! God's Word was sweet to me, its truths suddenly so clear. Quite spontaneously, it occurred to me that I should be baptised, which I was some weeks later. Church became home to me. The sudden change in my thinking and outlook gradually began to effect my behaviour, too.

However, this 'springtime' in my Christian experience did not last long. I continued to associate with my old friends and share in their activities. Within a year after my conversion, my joy and assurance of forgiveness had faded. During my first two years of high school, I experienced great inner conflict and misery, torn between a desire for secular pleasures and a longing for fellowship with the Lord. (Often, I would come home from having 'fun' at a party or dance and cry myself to sleep.)

The conflict finally ended when I went to Canada's Prairie Bible Institute for my third year of high school. There I realised that the root of my problem was that, although I was a Christian, I was geared to pleasing myself. In contrast, God's Word requires "that those who live should no longer live for themselves but for Him who died for them". Dutifully, I gave myself completely to the Lord. To my surprise, I found such joy in Him that, by comparison, the pleasures of the world were so flat and empty that they never lured me away again.

Not long after this commitment, the Lord opened my eyes to my personal responsibility for people without the gospel. In a conversation with my Bible teacher, I expressed my view that those who had never heard of Jesus would surely not be lost. By way of answer, he read Romans 10:13,14 to me: "Everyone who calls on the name of the Lord will be saved. How, then, can they call on the one they have not believed in? And how can they believe in the one of whom they have not heard?

And how can they hear without someone preaching to them?" The truth struck me like a slap in the face: they must hear to be saved. I must tell them!

Born a 'quitter'

In my last year of high school, the Lord laid Muslim people upon my heart. Through my Bible school years, I attended prayer meetings for Muslim lands, gathered material for private prayer and heard missionary speakers who worked with Muslims. I became aware of what a difficult work it was and what a special calibre of missionary it required. I had to admit, I wasn't the type. Persevering? Patient? I was a born 'quitter'. (As a child, I had never learned to roller skate because the first time I hit the hard pavement, I hurled the skates away, never to try again.) Giving up in the face of discouragement was a pattern in my life. If I was not meant to take the gospel to Muslims, then why this burden for them? "For prayer, of course," I concluded, and dropped the whole idea of being a missionary to them. However, no other people ever filled the place in my heart and prayers that the Muslims did.

When I went to the North American WEC headquarters as a missionary candidate in 1964, I had no idea what my field of service would be. As I considered various countries and prayed for guidance, I sought the counsel of an older, godly WEC staff member. "How do you recognise God's guidance?" Reflectively, he answered, "God's guidance is a quiet, persistent impression continuing over a long period of time." The only place to fit that description in my experience was the Muslim world.

As I reconsidered the possibility that God might want me there, the conviction grew that that was indeed His place for me. I could identify with the man with the withered hand. When Jesus asked him to stretch it out He was asking him to do exactly what he could not do! Yet his willingness to obey, and his confidence that if Jesus ordered it, He would make it possible, were the basis of a miracle. The Lord would do the same for me.

The quitter stays on

The work has been hard and discouraging. I have felt like quitting many times. The question, "What have we got to show for all our efforts?" has come many times. And each time the word would come, "Let us not become weary in doing good, for at the proper time we will reap a harvest if we do not give up" (Galatians 6:9). By God's grace, I am now in my twentieth year of service among Muslims, not planning to quit and still expecting to reap!

Another area of weakness was uncovered in my life after my first year of Bible school. As a lone Vacation Bible School teacher in the hills of Oklahoma, I experienced onslaughts of fear so severe that I was tempted to leave before my commitment was over. I have been vulnerable to fear ever since, but have repeatedly experienced the grace of God in this area too. The most notable example of this was during the Iranian Revolution.

When my husband and I left Iran in 1978 for a summer furlough, we were blissfully ignorant of the gathering political storm about to break over that land. In the ensuing months news reports caused us some concern; but we still did not take

the developments very seriously. Then, towards
the end of our time in the States, on a motel tele-
vision, we saw the image of a charred cinema in
Abadan where 1,000 people were burned to
death. That was in Iran, our 'home'! We realised
for the first time how grave was the situation.
Back in Switzerland (my husband's homeland), we
seriously weighed whether we should return with
our three blond children. Weeks of prayer
brought no new direction, which we understood
to mean that the plan to return to Iran was still
valid. Travelling overland, we arrived in Iran just
as the military took control of the country.

The next months were certainly adventurous:
street mobs, burning buildings, road barricades,
troop carriers rumbling down the streets, bullets
whizzing past the windows, public executions,
high-pitched anti-foreign propaganda, car bombs
in the shopping areas, Iraqi reconnaissance planes,
Iranian anti-aircraft artillery in the middle of the
night, a spy charge against our church, attempts
on the lives of the Anglican Bishop and his secretary, the murder of an Iranian pastor, imprison-
ment of three missionaries, and seething anti-
foreign feeling in some areas.

God's strength is sufficient

For me it was a blessing that we were so busy in
the Lord's work (and seeing such wonderful
things happen) that I hardly had time to dwell on
the dangers around us. But from time to time, the
thought would force itself upon me that we might
never get out of the country alive. Then I would
be so gripped by fear that I'd go trembling to my
room and fall on my knees before the Lord. My
cry was, "Lord, I don't want to leave this country

until it's Your will, but You see what a state I'm in. Please deliver me from my fears." With that, all fear would completely leave me. Thus we were able to stay on until our expulsion from the country in September 1980. I look upon those twenty-two months as the highlight of my life, not only for the unprecedented fruitfulness of our ministry during that period, but because I experienced the Lord's strength in my weakness as never before.

"I can do everything through Him who gives me strength." Yes, He gives strength to be a missionary, even a missionary to Muslims, even a missionary to Muslims in the midst of the Iranian Revolution!

Reflecting on the Lord's grace in the past makes me confident for the future. No matter what lies ahead, no matter how impossible it would be for me to cope by myself, His grace will be sufficient.

Points to Ponder:
1. Which term describes you better, 'quitter' or 'sticker'? What is the secret of stickability?
2. How do you cope with pressure? Is it right to ask to be saved from it?

Relevant scriptures:
1. 2 Corinthians 4:15-18.
2. Romans 5:3-5.

24

"YOU PRAY JUST LIKE YOUR MOTHER"

Jenny Faulkner

Fallen Angels

Missionaries' children . . . little angels? If so I was an exception to the rule, living in the Australian Western desert. I often think we were all more like *fallen* angels as we grew up during the succeeding years with our widowed mother. Dad had died soon after leaving the mission and there were no retirement plans for missionaries in those days. Mum's example of steadfastness and joy in very poor and difficult circumstances should have been enough to encourage us to follow her example, but my decision to be a Christian at the age of thirteen was motivated by a dread of missing out on something good, and an even stronger dread of hell.

From then on I set myself to live a good Christian life, expecting very high standards of myself and the others I was leading, first in high school, and then in my nursing training. But I rarely admitted inner failures and frustrations either to myself or to the others. I had a goal and was working hard to achieve it. I wanted to be matron of a mission hospital, so the plan was to finish nursing training and then go to Bible School. This goal was modified somewhat in 1968 when I met a

young man with the same background, upbringing and hang-ups that I had. But we also
shared the same ideals. I insisted on finishing my
nursing training and we married the month after.
Within a short time we moved to the very
Northernmost part of Western Australia, taking
on the pastoral care of an Aboriginal church.

Everything was difficult. The weather was un-
bearably hot. I wasn't matron of a hospital. I
wasn't even nursing. The town was full of people
who were kicking over the traces. The Aboriginal
people were easily led astray and there were no
mature Christians to whom we could turn for
help in our problems. In fact people came to us
with theirs! We soon discovered that the pat
answers we regurgitated from the experience of
others weren't satisfying to them or to us.

Removing the mask

We then began having problems of our own
because we began to see through the mask each
was wearing.

I refused to pray with my husband until one day
he asked me why. I told him, "I can't stand listening to your pious prayers any longer! You use
language that's your father's and it doesn't have
anything to do with the way you really feel."
Murray replied, "When you pray you sound just
like your mother!" That was the beginning of our
search for reality. We began to sort out all the
second-hand religion we had acquired from the
missionaries and retired workers amongst whom
we had lived. It was an absolute relief to be ourselves and begin again with our very own experience of the Lord.

With this discovery came a real desire to go on

with God, so Murray wrote to Stewart Dinnen, then Principal of the WEC Missionary Training College in Tasmania, asking for a more in-depth Bible study course than the one I had been using since before our marriage. In typical Stewart style, he just sent a prospectus for the next year's college intake! For us, Missionary Training College seemed like heaven after two years of the simple choruses and children's stories that we had used for illiterate Aborigines. And of course we were desperate for answers to some of the problems we had seen on the mission scene.

God changes real people

I remember Stewart's question to me after we had been at MTC for several months. "Whatever happened to the irrepressible Jenny Mack?" (as I had been when first introduced to him three years earlier). Not only my name had changed; the self-confident, self-sufficient upstart personality had been changed too. The process had started in Kununurra in Western Australia but continued during our time at Missionary Training College.

In the second year I saw the Lord moulding the Murray I had known into the building supervisor, senior student, Sunday School superintendent and co-pastor, all at the same time. And I had to find my place working with this transformed person! My acceptance of his leadership was quite a struggle, but the rewards it brought far outweighed the trials. As I look back over the lessons we have learned together, I see the blessing I have received from being allowed to share in the deepest struggles he has passed through, and from which he has emerged victorious. I know that my opinion is desired and valued, even though the final word in decisions is his.

Coping with childlessness

Towards the end of our Candidate Course en route to Brazil, our Australian leader gave us some fatherly counsel. After asking us carefully about our childless state, he warned us that this issue could become a pressure point, even though it was not at that time. He was right, of course. At first it wasn't difficult, even with the point-blank questions we were often asked by the Brazilians. "Why don't you have any children?" "Don't you like them?" "What are you doing to avoid having children?" Our stock answer became, "Yes, we do like children but we're just slow learners!" That usually produced a good laugh and a welcome change of subject.

It was hard to cope with the uncertainty regarding pregnancy. No medical person had ever said that there was no possibility of my having children. After ten years of marriage I sought help, mostly to satisfy my curiosity, but also because I thought I would regret it later if I had not done my part. There were tests and operations, which were a strain physically as well as psychologically. Without spelling it out, I had felt a misfit for quite some time, because I was no longer single, nor a young woman. It meant I had no talking point with the Brazilian women who talk 'children' all the time. As a midwife, I could talk about births from a second-hand point of view but there it stopped. Neither did I seem to be able to resolve the problem of whether I needed to pray for healing or not, because I was never really sure if that was what the Lord wanted. Most of the time I thoroughly enjoyed being able to accompany Murray in his work and had no real burning desire to have children, except for the odd occasion when I did want to be a mother and to give Murray a child.

In acceptance lies peace

Eventually I saw that having passed through all this, I was able to help other women with the same problem: the fear of the word 'sterility', the option of adoption and the fears that that brings, to say nothing of the uncertainty, lack of faith for healing, and the misunderstandings of others. For me the lesson is, 'In acceptance lies peace.' Whether that peace is for always depends on accepting God's sovereign plan for me personally, not whether I have children or not.

Whilst having treatment in South Africa, I was given a verse especially for me, "He settles the barren woman in her home as a happy mother of children" (Psalm 113:9). Is that a physical family or a spiritual one? I don't really know yet, but I am the happy mother of 'children' and 'grandchildren' at the Brazilian Bible School in Montes Claros, and I have discovered the truth of peace through acceptance.

Points to Ponder:
1. What aspects of your spiritual life would you call second hand (i.e. conforming to another's pattern), and what aspects would you call genuine?
2. 'In acceptance lies peace.' Is this a Biblical concept? Does it need to be qualified in any way?

Relevant scriptures:
1. Philippians 3:3-6.
2. 1 Peter 5:5-7, 1 Timothy 6:11-12.

25

PRUNING AND STRETCHING

Nan Pin Chee

An imp and an idol worshipper

Growing up in a rural tin-mining village, with eight other brothers and sisters, made for an interesting life. My parents were busy earning enough to feed and clothe us. Often we had to fend for ourselves against other children in the community. In a multicultural society such as Malaysia, it is not hard to make friends with Malay and Indian children, and to learn their culture and traditions. My parents brought their ancestral worship with them when they migrated to Malaysia from China, so we were deeply involved in the worship of idols.

I was a reluctant student at the start of my schooling. My mother had to sit in class to keep me in school! In Malaysia, the social pressure is such that in order to gain acceptance a person has either to be rich or well-educated. Since we couldn't be rich, my family decided that the second option was viable. This could be one of the reasons why they sent me to a Catholic secondary school for my education. I studied the Gospel of Mark as a class subject and gained reasonable marks, but no one explained to me the significance of the person Jesus.

Malaysia to New Zealand

After finishing at high school, I was accepted

for further education in New Zealand. I took up this opportunity with great expectation. The whole world was opening up before me. But God had another plan. During the first year of university, I discovered that much knowledge was not the answer to life, but was in fact 'a weariness to the flesh'. I began to search for the meaning of life and was converted as a result of accepting persistent invitations to a Christian fellowship.

When I was finishing my studies, the Lord spoke to me about Bible college training, and I was introduced to missionary work by a member of WEC. In 1976 I was married to the most beautiful girl in the world, and we both joined WEC in 1980. Initially, we went to Singapore, but after the government refused to grant us residence permits, the Lord opened the door for us to go to Hong Kong, and we have been there since 1982. Here are some of the lessons the Lord has taught us along the way.

A perplexing situation

God is concerned with the fruitfulness of His workers and increases our effectiveness both by pruning (as in John 15) and by stretching. This is 'on-the-job' training, and sometimes the stretching and pruning may be too intense for comfort! But this is the best way of learning spiritual truth. Let me illustrate from our experience.

People often ask us how we ended up in Hong Kong. The truth of the matter is that we had no choice. We were so fixed in our mind about Singapore that Hong Kong was not even a vague possibility.

After finishing our Candidate Course and spending a year at the Missionary Training College in

Tasmania, we went to Singapore. Our goal was to help another couple in the work of challenging Asians to cross-cultural evangelism. We fitted into the Singapore scene. We experienced a minimal amount of cultural shock and opportunities came to present the missionary challenge in numerous churches. We could see the possibility of commencing a candidates orientation course, and even expanding WEC representation to neighbouring countries. As far as we were concerned, we were ready to serve there until the Lord led us on, but we never expected that to be so soon after our arrival.

We found it more and more difficult to renew our residence permits as each month passed by. Finally, at the end of four months, the immigration authority asked us to leave the country within four weeks. Many prayed, and repeated appeals were made for a reversal of the decision, but to no avail. We had to leave. Two choices were before us — to go back to New Zealand, or to another field. But where? Just before we received the refusal, my wife woke up early one morning obviously alarmed by what the Lord had revealed to her during her sleep. "Last night," she said, "I saw that we were in a devastating financial situation; but before this picture went away, a voice spoke, 'My God shall supply all your need.'" We prayed together that if this was from the Lord, He would confirm it; if not, we asked that He would remove it from our mind. This promise kept us going through difficult situations which lay ahead of us. We were prepared to move when the final appeal was rejected, although we were perplexed. Was our guidance to Singapore wrong?

Then the invitation to Hong Kong came, and

my wife and I had peace. We knew that was the place for us. The move from Singapore was a seeming setback as far as we were concerned, but a step forward in God's plan for Hong Kong. He was able to use us to strengthen the work there and see it emerge as a missionary sending base. His timing was right, because many Christians were ready to launch out into cross-cultural evangelism, and WEC became one of the channels for them.

God had to close the door to work in Singapore because there was no other way that He could draw our attention to Hong Kong. We had spiritual blinkers on. The way that the Lord removed our short-sightedness was painful, but very effective.

Nothing wasted in God's economy

Our short stay in Singapore wasn't for nothing. It prepared us for a new life style, the so-called 'compact style of living' of Hong Kong, where the average living space is about one-third of the size of Western houses. We would have had some major adjustments to make if we had been thrown straight from New Zealand into these high-rise apartments. It doesn't bother us now when the whole block sways during a typhoon, or that the tables and chairs have to be folded up and put away when not in use. Hong Kong is home for us and a land of harvest. God not only opens the door, He also prepares the workers to fit the task.

The first few months in Hong Kong were another stage in God's training programme. Faith was top of the list. We read about men and women of faith; we had heard dozens of sermons on it and even preached on it. But when we came to the situation where we had to exercise it, that was different! One of the most difficult and yet common areas of faith is that of finance. The Lord must have known that we needed to be stretched in this area.

Following the expense of moving from Singapore to Hong Kong, securing accommodation, and having other unforeseen expenses, we experienced our first financial crisis. It was around the Chinese New Year festival. The price of meat and vegetables went higher and higher as the festival drew nearer. We wondered how we were going to get by. One afternoon, we had a visit from a couple who had been trying to settle here, and were finding it difficult to make ends meet. We had a good time as they shared about their situation and we prayed together. As the afternoon went on, the Lord spoke to me about giving them our housekeeping money for the next two weeks. Inwardly, I tried to reason with God that we shouldn't. Even when they were leaving and walking out of the door, I was still debating about whether to give it or not. My wife whispered that we should help our friends. Without further hesitation, I pressed our gift into their hands just before the doors of the lift closed. We were poor but happy.

The day before the festival I was waiting for the lift, to go down to the bank to draw out the last hundred Hong Kong dollars (about 10 pounds sterling), and was surprised to see this same friend stepping out of the lift. Handing me an envelope, he said, "Thanks for your gift. We have something for you too. Happy New Year." We praised God, for in that envelope was ten times the amount we had given them!

We learned that in order to free the Lord to work in our lives, He requires obedience. The boy with five loaves and two fishes never thought that through his simple and yet significant step of giving, the Lord would be able to work a miracle. For us, the Lord surely did supply all our need. He wants us to learn to walk by faith and not by sight.

We Chinese don't kiss

Many missionaries suffer culture shock, but I had my main dose while in New Zealand before the candidates orientation course. Through that experience, the Lord showed me that no cultural difference is too great to surmount, and He helped me to adjust in a marvellous way.

In a traditional Chinese family, physical expressions of love and appreciation are seldom displayed; a handshake is the limit. On first arriving in New Zealand, I was no different. Being an overseas student, I hadn't many opportunities to be introduced to the more intimate side of New Zealand's culture. Anyway, who wants to kiss a Chinese on the cheek, let alone hug him? Even after I became a Christian, the church which I was attending did not take Paul's exhortation 'to greet one another with a holy kiss' literally. But this state of tranquility was not to last for ever.

We used to make regular trips to see my in-laws in a nearby town. My father-in-law is a retired farmer, who takes great delight in shocking and teasing others. In this town there was a well-built, motherly lady who attended the Salvation Army, and her love for the Lord was matched only by her dedication to hugging God's people. Whenever she was introduced to other Christians she would grab them and hug them till all the air was squeezed out of their lungs. My father-in-law was keen for me to get the full treatment! I didn't know what to expect, but was looking forward to seeing this well-known character.

One of the local weekend attractions in this small town was the flea market, a group of stalls selling just about anything from handcrafts to home baking. We visited the market one Saturday morning. As we went round my father-in-law was right in his element, greeting different friends. Suddenly he spoke to this lady who was looking after a book stall. "Hazel, this is my son-in-law who is going to be a missionary." The lady responded and in spite of her bulk moved effortlessly around the table. The crowd moved aside; it was like the parting of the Red Sea. So this was the lady I had to meet! I put out my hand for a handshake. She did not just put out one hand, but both hands. She was going to hug me! ("Oh Lord, not here, not in front of this crowd!") Now I understand why some hugs are called 'bear hugs'. She hung on for what seemed an eternity, and even planted a kiss on my cheek. Is that what Paul called 'a holy kiss'? In the confusion, she said, "Isn't Jesus wonderful? I love you, brother. God bless you." I was speechless as she expressed her love in such a manner, oblivious of the crowd looking on. She accepted me, a stranger, as a brother in the Lord, and I was touched. I found myself muttering "I love you too, sister," and I meant it.

I have read and heard about many ways in which God broke the mould of a missionary's upbringing, so that a bridge of friendship could be built in a different culture. The Lord certainly did that for me that winter morning. The memory has helped me through many cross-cultural situations since.

As I continue in my walk with the Lord, my prayer is, "Lord, I am still in the kindergarten department of Your training school, but I want to go on with You; make me what You want me to be."

Points to Ponder:
1. Have you ever experienced God closing one door and opening another for you? What was the result in your spiritual life?
2. How do you *demonstrate* God's love? Should you?

Relevant scriptures:
1. 1 Corinthians 16:19, 2 Corinthians 2:12.
2. 1 Timothy 1:5.

26

THE LOGICAL THING TO DO

Liz Hentschel

No Alternative

"How did God call you to be a missionary in Spain?"

"Well ... uh ... He didn't."

"What?"

"In a sense, I became one out of ignorance." (Quizzical looks all round.)

My evangelical background was virtually nil, so when I became a Christian a whole new adventure opened up before me. The friends who had shown me how I could know Jesus were all nurses who were heading for Bible college and the mission field. I, too, was a Christian and a nurse. It therefore seemed the most logical thing in the world to follow their example. To me there was no alternative. (Oh ignorant bliss!)

Interest in Spain grew over the years, especially after I heard of its resistance to the good news about Jesus. I decided to head in that direction. Can I remember spending hours in prayer waiting for the Lord to say, "Liz, I want you in Spain"? No. The interest was mine, and I told the Lord that that was where I wanted to go. Perhaps my ideas for finding guidance were a little unorthodox but, nevertheless, here I am in Spain today, thoroughly convinced that I didn't miss God's way.

Jesus said, "*Go* and make disciples of all

nations," and as far as I was concerned, unless He told me to stop heading for Spain, then I would crash on. There was a sneaking suspicion, however, that my desire to go was directly in line with the Lord's desires.

Flopped Ministries Inc.

The FMI could well be the name of my business if ever I were to start one: Flopped Ministries Incorporated. Not that I didn't do well at school or in my training as a nurse and midwife. Nor was my childhood anything out of the ordinary: 'helping' my Dad to harvest the wheat, picnics in the 'bush' with my family, in with the 'in' crowd at high school. At one stage life became a round of parties. Outwardly, people saw a lively, smiling teenager, but inwardly I knew the truth. I was popular, and yet desperately lonely. Exuberant and happy on the outside, I was inwardly longing for that elusive something to fill my life, something more than froth and bubble. Despite relative success in education and career, I felt my life was a flop, in that I could do nothing right. I was inferiority complex personified. Had I somehow slipped into the human race when God wasn't looking? I felt so at times.

The failure complex seeped into my Christian experience as well. Though I was all fired up to dash off and serve the Lord, I hadn't realised that some very fundamental changes had to take place in my life first. The Lord had to lasso me and teach me some thrilling truths. But the day came when He released me for service.

Seething in Spain

The time? Two o'clock in the morning. The

date? May 6, 1979. The place? Madrid airport. As I stepped from the plane — albeit in a jet-lagged stupor — my missionary career began. I arrived with the truths that the Father had taught me tucked away tightly in my heart. Nothing could wrench these from their position. But little did I realise exactly what was in store.

All manner of nasty little 'beasties' start to surface when one is under pressure. After the novelty of the new setting wore off, I began to experience the pressure that missionaries are under. I could feel those beastly carnal reactions stirring within, and the largest was resentment.

"Liz, so-and-so reports that you've said such-and-such," a fellow worker accused one day, obviously upset that I'd said such a thing. Self-defence welled up and spilled out. "I have never said any such thing!" I blurted. The seed of resentment started to germinate. How dare she say that? Now she's got me into trouble! I felt like punching her lights out!

Then there was the male missionary who implied that single girls are put on this earth as etceteras — that they're good for nothing except doing the wives' housework and looking after other people's children. Pride was added to the resentment. Nasty mixture! Who does he think he is? He has no right to treat *me* like that! Lying in bed at night seething, I worked out all sorts of disagreeable retorts. My inside churned around — stomach ulcer, here I come! Resentment was blooming nicely, and no doubt the devil was happy with his work.

Other situations where I'd been hurt pushed their way up into my consciousness. Hurt, hurt, and more hurt. Resentment and pride had laid a

suitable bed for the seeds of bitterness, a real
killer of spiritual vitality and effectiveness. The
choice hit me head on. Choose to forgive and be
free, or choose not to forgive and remain tangled
up, a missionary in name only, with my relationship with the Father and with others greatly
impaired. A simple choice in a way, but a costly
one to make. Would I forgive? What a traumatic
day it was, hiding away on my own, asking the
Lord to show me those I needed to forgive. Scene
after scene flashed into my mind and tore at my
heart as I remembered how deeply I'd been hurt.

"Lord, I forgive him." "I forgive her." Some I
balked at. "Oh no! You're not asking me to forgive
them? Don't You remember how they treated me?"
He did, of course, and still He asked me to forgive.
In fact, He had me cornered. There was no
alternative. I caught glimpses of how the Father
could have felt as He stood back and watched His
Son mocked, wounded and killed. If He forgave, I
had to do the same. How does one measure tears?
By the handkerchief full? In my case, that day, it
seemed by the bath full!

That was it, then. No more problems with resentment? Wrong! My arch enemy, the devil,
knows where I'm likely to trip. He knows me fairly
well because I used to be on his side. However, as
a lady once demanded as she prayed with me, I
say, "Satan, you can just go jump in the lake of
fire!" People, often without knowing it, continue
to hurt me. That's all part of life. Those little
niggles of resentment aren't always dealt with in
the right manner or as quickly as they should be.
They don't come clearly labelled, "With love from
the devil."

Working with God becomes exciting

May is show time in my home town. What fun it used to be to run from one sideshow ride to another. The ferris wheel as a starter, a relatively smooth ride which promised your inside more to come. Then came the 'cha cha' which began the serious work of jostling every internal organ from its rightful position. For the grand finale, there was the 'octopus' ride where one is spun in the car, lifted, dropped and rotated simultaneously. I well remember that sense of anticipation in my stomach on the day of the show. Over the last few years, I've realised that the Christian life doesn't have to be stodgy. Just as I used to be excited about those rides back home, in Spain I'm getting excited about new facets of God's character. They were there all the time, of course. I just wasn't looking!

There was the time a pastor's wife asked me to pray with her because she really wanted to know God experientially. She already knew all the head stuff! I literally sat back and watched the Holy Spirit reveal to that dear woman exactly what we had asked. A church deacon, stuck for years in a traditional rut, suddenly blossomed in his relationship with Jesus. A young lad was freed from demons. A thirty-five-year-old lady wept uncontrollably over a cup of coffee, as she realised for the first time that Jesus really loved her. An old widow walked three kilometres from her home in search of the evangelical church, pouring out her tragic story and reaching out to Jesus.

Some nights I lie in bed too excited to sleep. "Lord, why don't You have a day off tomorrow? If You don't hold off for a while, I'll burst!" Mind you, if truth be known, there's no way I want Him to stop!

Coping with the dull days

Of course, some days are dull; in fact, they are downright depressing. There are antagonistic doorkeepers who won't let you into their blocks of apartments. One refused to let me in, so I sneaked through when a tenant came out, and shoved literature into the fifty or so letter boxes at lightning speed. I was all set for a hasty escape, but soon discovered that the main door couldn't be opened from the inside without a key! There I stood, trying desperately to make myself invisible in the shadows, fearing the doorkeeper would come out of her ground-floor apartment and give me a piece of her mind. Minutes dragged by and then another tenant came down and unlocked the door. I almost bowled her over as I burst through!

Cristina had told me to go back to visit her any time, that her home was my home. Why then didn't she even open the door the next time I went? Then there was the ill-tempered fellow who pushed me out of the way as I tried to witness to him. And Manolo, a heroin addict who was only out to get our money (the spiritual interest was no more than a facade). To think that I had trusted him! There was Pilar: despite repeated explanations of a simple Bible passage, she still couldn't grasp its significance. And the hours spent at the park where the only ones who would listen to me were the dogs and the trees!

I am sure you have heard this style of testimony: "Since knowing Jesus I've been so happy." Well, sometimes I've never been so depressed! But please don't misunderstand what I'm saying.

This is what I'm getting at: "It's tough being a missionary, Father. But, it's been in those states of discouragement and depression when I've yelled

'Help!' that You've come running and shown me more of Your lovely Self. I wouldn't have missed that for anything. I do miss family, physical comforts, my home church (so loving, and growing by leaps and bounds) and friends. But no, I wouldn't have missed this for anything."

Points to Ponder:
1. Are you holding resentment against anyone? What is the Biblical way of dealing with the problem?
2. What is your response to the command of Jesus, "Go into all the world and preach the gospel to all creation"?

Relevant scriptures:
1. Matthew 18:15-22, Matthew 5:43-44.
2. Isaiah 2:8-10, Romans 1:14-16.

If you are interested in Christian service, write to:

WEC International, Bulstrode, Gerrards Cross, Bucks, SL9 8SZ, UK.

OR:

WEC International, 48 Woodside Avenue, Strathfield, NSW 2135, Australia.

WEC International, 37 Aberdeen Avenue, Hamilton, Ontario, L8P 2N6, Canada.

WEC International, PO Box 27264, Mt Roskill, Auckland 4, New Zealand.

WEC International, PO Box 47777, Greyville, 4023, Republic of South Africa.

WEC International, Box 1707, Fort Washington, PA 19034, USA.